SUNDERLAND

the making of a 21st century city

Written by Carol Roberton

Edited by Dr Colin Sinclair

Preface by Kate Adie

This book is a joint publication by the City of Sunderland and the Sunderland Echo.

1st Edition 2000

Published by Chief Executive's Department, City of Suncerland.
Designed and produced by NB Group Ltd, Gateshead.

Hardback: ISBN 0 9537937 0 2
Paperback: ISBN 0 9537937 1 0

preface

You never lose your roots. Not if you come from Sunderland. From Sarajevo to Delhi to Beijing, I've been greeted with the words – You're from Sunderland – and to the puzzlement of my friends and colleagues, discussed streets and schools and the state of the football team with complete strangers. Except they're not strangers, because they're from Sunderland.

What is it about a town that sits a bit apart on the north-east coast? A place of shipyards and glassworks and coal and The Lads?

For me, it was a safe place to grow up, where you went across the river on the way to a glorious beach and a shivering dip at Seaburn. The river was a place of smoke and metal clanging, as the ships emerged to carry the town's name across the world. We ran around Tunstall Hills as children, to see the whole place spread out below us, living history, where almost everyone could point out their street, see the river cranes, Penshaw Monument, the church spires of confident Victorians. It was our town and it felt like one big family. A place where shopping is something that you do in between meeting people.

A town with a modest claim to history – the first glass made in England, the citizens declaring from Cromwell, home to Jack Crawford of Camperdown, and with a marvellous stuffed walrus dominating the Museum. The Empire Theatre, where I'd been one of the entranced four-year-olds, lured on stage by Dick Whittington's prancing cat to sing terribly. Roker Park, where I was a teenage Paddock-ite, part of the Roar for Cloughie and Charlie Hurley.

And a town to come back to, even through the tough years of industrial decline, and to see, slowly, a regeneration. Now a city. A new life growing up again round the river. A university, a centre for glass, a new football stadium. The Venerable Bede, looking up from learning his Latin in St Peter's would recognise the place, a river curling through a hive of work, peopled by decent, canny folk.

Kate Adie

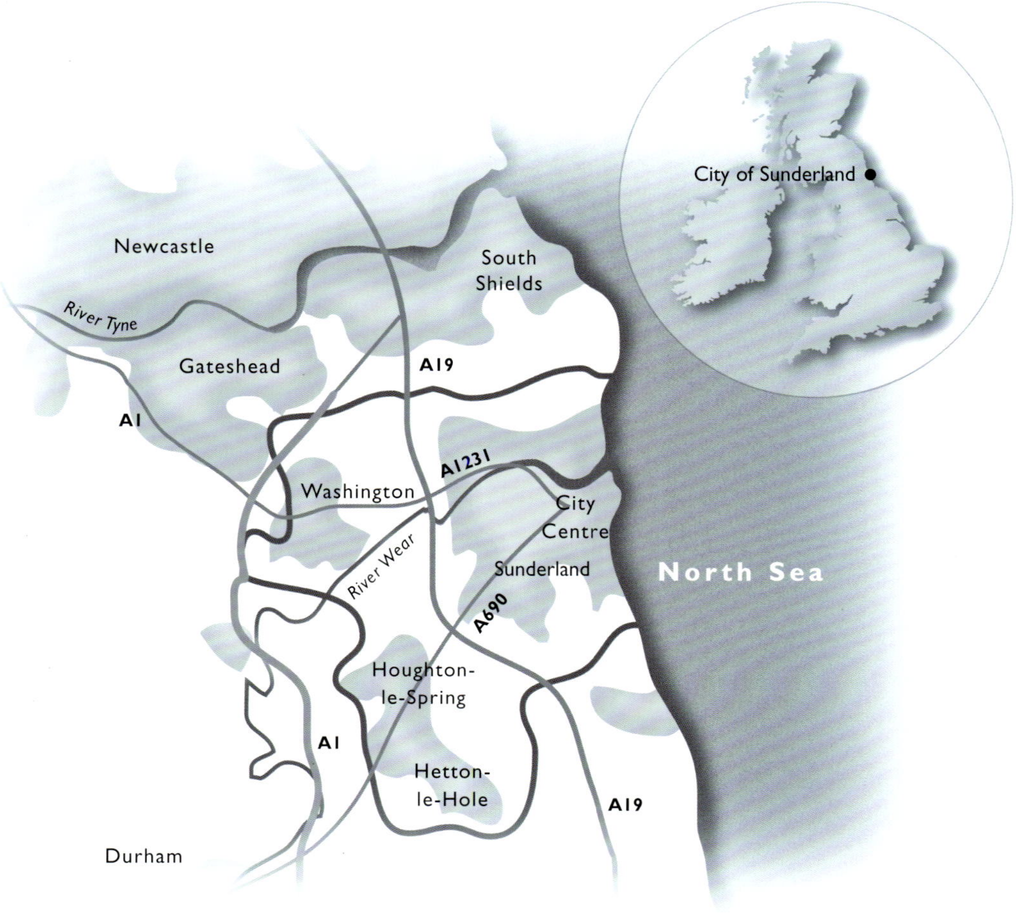

CITY OF SUNDERLAND

foreword

This book celebrates more than 2,000 years in the development of the City of Sunderland. It looks back with pride on the successes of the past – achieved often in the face of adversity – and forward to an exciting new future as the city undergoes one of the greatest transformations in its history.

Our book highlights the way in which evidence of the past colours our landscape today. From the signs of prehistory in landmarks like Claxheugh Rock, and the first marks of early man, to the urban developments of the great Victorian industrialists, to the present day. And it looks at the way in which new landmarks, like the Stadium of Light, are fast becoming new symbols for our city. The stadium, built on the site of the former Wearmouth Colliery, embodies the spirit of change taking place here. It projects a strong sense of Sunderland's past, while at the same time testifying to our city's promising future.

As we move forward into the new Millennium, Sunderland is reaching back to its roots. When he built St Peter's Monastery on the banks of the Wear, Sunderland's founding father Benedict Biscop established a centre of learning and industry which was to become famous throughout the world. His pioneering lead helped to take the city forward then and is still very much part of our culture and economy today.

This same site is now home to Sunderland University's St Peter's Campus – a modern cathedral of learning with the latest technology and banks of computers making knowledge accessible to people of all ages. Nearby the new National Glass Centre, dedicated to the art and industry of glassmaking, celebrates the craft Benedict Biscop brought to our city more than 1,300 years ago.

Above all, our book celebrates the human spirit and the way in which the sense of community forged in the hard times of the past survives in the spirit of Sunderland today.

For at this time of change, the city continues to draw on its most important asset – its people. The people from the former coalfield communities such as Hetton and Houghton, from Washington New Town and the old town of Sunderland, have come together to present a powerful new face to the world and they colour the new and developing city with their experiences and heritage. This book is dedicated to them.

Dr Colin Sinclair
Chief Executive, City of Sunderland

contents

chapter one

Golden Age

A sculpture in stone and inlaid stained glass, outside the University of Sunderland's St Peter's Campus, representing books produced by Wearmouth's seventh century monks.

STONE BOOKS

The golden age of Wearmouth began at the end of the seventh century when a young nobleman called Benedict Biscop established a monastery on the riverside which was to have an enduring influence on the whole of civilisation.

St Peter's became one of the greatest centres of learning in medieval Christendom. Scholars and travellers came from all over Europe to visit. With its twin, St Paul's, of Jarrow, it has been nominated for World Heritage Site status for it was to be the birthplace of ideas which have an impact on life today. The work of the Venerable Bede, its greatest son, is still available in many languages.

It was on his return from a pilgrimage to Rome that Biscop, born in 627 at the Royal Court of Northumbria, was given 15 square miles of land at the mouth of the River Wear to found a monastery in 673. Later, he was given another strip of land across the river. It is thought that this land "sundered" from the main monastery gave Sunderland its name. So in two ways we could look to Benedict Biscop as our founding father and following the city status granted to Sunderland in 1992 and the consecration of former Bishopwearmouth Parish Church as a Minster, he was chosen to be our patron saint.

The wonder of local people as the great monastery was built can only be guessed at. They were living in houses of mud and wattle and had forgotten how to work in stone and glass. The trappings of civilisation brought by the Romans were long gone.

Existing churches and monasteries, like Lindisfarne, were made of wood. But Benedict (also known as Benet, hence St Benet's Church at Monkwearmouth) wanted buildings in the Romanesque style he had seen on his European travels.

He brought stonemasons from France to create decorative carved stone and Gallic glassmakers to create beautiful stained glass windows. He commissioned paintings so people unable to read could have direct access to Gospel stories.

The Archanter John came from the Vatican to teach Gregorian chant. St Peter's was established as a centre of music.

Benedict built up a great library. Copies were made of religious and secular books to augment those brought back from his travels. Soon the scriptorium was turning out its own decorative manuscripts and later, there were the works of Bede to keep them busy.

After Benedict's death, the library was expanded by Abbot Ceolfrid and the scriptorium's most famous work, the Codex Amiatinus, known as the Wearmouth Bible, was produced. Ceolfrid had three copies made, one each for Wearmouth and Jarrow, which were lost, and one for Rome, which he took with him on his last journey. The manuscript is now in the Laurentian Library in Florence.

All the important figures in medieval Christendom walked through the Anglo-Saxon arch into St Peter's, which became a parish church when the monastery closed in 1536.

Opposite: One of three stained glass windows in St Peter's Church, created by Leonard Evetts. The window shows Benedict Biscop carrying an abbot's crook and a container, possibly of relics.

ST PETER'S CHURCH

Bede, universally recognised as the greatest European scholar of the early Middle Ages, is Wearside's most famous son. He has been called "the father of English history" and "the early morning star of English literature". He is both these things and much more, a great scholar not only of his own time, but of all time.

His Ecclesiastical History, which told the story of Britain's conversion to Christianity, was the first book to promote the concept of the English as a nation. Much of his other work had a universal appeal and is still available in many languages all over the world today.

> Before the inevitable journey no one can be
> So wise that for him it will not be necessary
> To consider before his going hence
> What for his soul of good or ill
> After his death day the judgement will be
>
> Bede's Death Song

He is renowned for his work on time. Most Anglo-Saxons lived according to "seasonal" days whose length varied according to the time of year, but Bede introduced the 24-hour day.

And but for Bede we might not have celebrated the Millennium. In his day, several different calendars were in operation and in many places the passage of time was counted by the number of years their ruler had been in charge. Bede adopted and popularised the system of taking the birth of Christ as the great divide in time, and counting years either by their number Before Christ (BC) or after, Anno Domini (AD) or Year of Our Lord. Bede used this system in his Ecclesiastical History, others followed and the use of this method of counting time was an important unifying factor in Europe. So it is that we come to the 21st century.

Bede was a great populariser and aimed to use language to which his readers could relate. Even in translation into modern English, his words paint vivid pictures and his images from everyday life convey difficult concepts. For example, in trying to convey the brevity of one person's life in relation to time, he uses the image of the king sitting with his thanes at dinner on a winter's day and says life is "like the swift flight of a sparrow through the banqueting hall". Inside, there is a comforting fire, outside the storms of winter rain are raging.

Bede was a poet as well as a writer and historian, and though his poetry, like all his other work, was devoted to the service of Christ, he sometimes used the style of Anglo-Saxon secular poetry, as in the poem known as "Bede's Death Song".

Above all, Bede wanted to increase levels of understanding. He translated the Creed and the Lord's Prayer into Old English so people who were not fluent in Latin could understand what they were saying in their prayers.

Icon of the Venerable Bede, greatest European scholar of medieval times, and Sunderland's most famous son.

Opposite: Bede's Death Song.

BEDE ICON

While his work travelled far and wide, Bede himself, so far as we know, never travelled further than Lindisfarne or York – though this did not prevent him from composing a book on the holy places of Palestine. For he gathered a vast base of knowledge and produced large numbers of text books across a wide range of subjects for his pupils – computation and astronomy as well as history and literature. Here was someone who embodied the concept of "Renaissance Man" a Millennium before the Renaissance.

The aspect of Bede's work which most impressed his contemporaries was his commentary on the Scriptures. The huge reputation of St Cuthbert throughout the Christian world explains the number of manuscripts of Bede's two versions of his life, one in prose and the other in Latin verse. Locally, his History of the Abbots is important as it describes the foundation of Wearmouth and Jarrow by Benedict Biscop.

But it is as a historian that Bede is most famous today, and in particular for his Ecclesiastical History. The two great eighth century manuscripts of this work are known respectively as the Moore Bede, which is in Cambridge, and the Leningrad Bede, in St Petersburg.

And it is worth remembering the adverse circumstances in which he worked. In a letter to Lull of Mainz, the Abbot Cuthbert of Wearmouth apologises for the small number of Bede's works he was able to send – for the bitter weather had seized the hand of the scribe.

He studied the constellations and produced a method for computing the date of Easter, and from data collected by monks in a number of coastal monasteries, he drew up a method for predicting tides on a 19-year lunar cycle. His aim was to build up a clear picture of the physical world around him.

Yet we know remarkably little of his own life. Historians are even in dispute about whether he ever lived at St Paul's, Jarrow, though a museum has been created in his honour on the site of the monastery there. We do know he was born in 672 or 673 and given at the age of seven to be educated by abbot Benedict Biscop, who by then had founded the monastery of St Peter's at Wearmouth. He was made a deacon at 19 and ordained a priest at the age of 30.

Bede died in 735 and later in the eighth century, the Viking raids started. The country lapsed into chaos. The great days of Wearmouth were certainly over. In the ninth century, the Danes arrived and Northumbria ceased to be an English kingdom. The monasteries at Wearmouth and Jarrow lay in ruins. They were restored in 1075 by a Benedictine called Aldwine, but in 1083 became simply cells of Durham. In 1536, Wearmouth closed and St Peter's became a parish church as it remains today.

The unveiling ceremony of Bede's Cross in 1904 conducted by the Archbishop of York. Sculpted by G.W. Milburn of York, the intricate stonework depicts the life of the Venerable Bede. The cross stands sentinel on Cliffe Park overlooking Roker.

Opposite: Death scene, detail from Bede's Cross.

BEDE'S CROSS

Stained glass made by Sunderland craftsmen using hand-blown techniques little changed from Saxon times, graces cathedrals and major buildings all over the world. The technique used by the Gallic glassblowers brought to Wearmouth by Biscop in the seventh century was developed and perfected in the 19th century and carried on, with only slight concessions to modern technology, by the Hartley Wood company almost to the end of the 20th century.

The company, whose antique glass had a stunning visual appeal, became a world-leader, and we have some of the finest examples of it on Wearside. It was used in the great churches built in the 19th century – like Christ Church and St Mark's – as the population of the old town moved south and west. It also appears in many windows in Durham Cathedral and projects as diverse as Castletown Primary School, the restored Rose Line building at Wylam Wharf, and Aykley Heads House, Durham.

The last great local church project using Hartley Wood glass was to renew the windows of St Nicholas' Church. It was regarded by experts as the best work of the 20th century's finest glass artist, Leonard Evetts, who died in 1997. From 1963 to 1992, he created 46 stained glass masterpieces for the church, a project of the magnitude of the work of the medieval artists he admired.

This continuing tradition – as well as being the place stained glassmaking was introduced in Britain – was critical to Sunderland's success in becoming the National Glass Centre.

The stunning £17million centre is itself a monument to glass with its vast glass roof and walls of glass overlooking the river. Inside, visitors can see demonstrations of glassblowing as part of a glass tour and in the shop, buy examples of glass made both here and at other centres of excellence in Britain. As well as the permanent Kaleidoscope Gallery, which illustrates the various wonders of glass, there is also a gallery for short-term exhibitions of glass.

The centre has helped to put Sunderland back on the cultural and tourist maps of Britain. At the end of the first year, in June 1999, more than 150,000 people had visited the National Glass Centre. Between them they had bought more than 50,000 marbles and thousands of vases and bowls. And 73,000 lunches had been eaten in the prestigious restaurant.

The centre hosted the first British Glassmaking Showcase and was also cited as one of the reasons that Sunderland was chosen to host Europe's first Creative Summit, a three-day international event for the arts and media.

The National Glass Centre stands on the riverside close to the place Gallic craftsmen introduced glassblowing to Britain in the seventh century.

Opposite: A stained glass window in St. Nicholas' Church created by Leonard Evetts.

NATIONAL GLASS CENTRE

A sculpture of stone books with an inlaid mosaic of stained glass, representing the decorative manuscripts created by the monks of St Peter's in the seventh century, symbolises the way a full circle has been turned on the riverside site which was one of the greatest centres of learning in medieval Christendom. For the sculpture lies outside the fine buildings of the University of Sunderland's St Peter's Campus, the new centre of learning now occupying the site of the great monastery.

Since its opening in 1995, the award-winning multi-million pound campus has been at the forefront of new systems of learning and working, with initiatives like the Informatics Centre, a "computer cathedral" open to business and industry as well as students and staff. The university itself is big business, with an annual turnover of £63million, 15,000 full and part-time students, 1,000 international students, and national excellence ratings in media studies, biological sciences, physiology, pharmacy and pharmacology.

And now, led by its chancellor, the Oscar-winning producer Lord Puttnam, the university has unveiled a vision of the future which would see Sunderland as an international power-house for the creative industries. It will centre on a new School of Arts, Media and Design, housing an art gallery and auditorium to become a centre for excellence in the arts and a major asset for the people of Sunderland. It has the backing of industrialists in the region and the university intends to sell some of its older prestigious buildings to help pay for it. This will consolidate its teaching on two sites, the other being the Chester Road development which grew from the old municipal technical college established in Green Terrace in 1901 and the nucleus of further and higher education in Sunderland.

The tech became the first English college to introduce the sandwich course, with alternating periods of learning and working. From the start, like the university today, it was committed to lifelong learning and to widening participation in education in the local community, with evening classes opening up new paths. In 1969, it became one of the first three polytechnics in Britain and it became a university in 1992, the year Sunderland gained city status.

Throughout, there has been a tradition of serving the local community and providing local people with the skills needed for local industry. Formerly this meant fields like mining, mechanical and marine engineering. Now Lord Puttnam believes that the centre for the arts will be a catalyst for change in the entire city, placing the creative industries at its heart in the way that heavy industries were in the past.

Fine new buildings of the award-winning St Peter's Campus of the University of Sunderland occupy the riverside site where St Peter's Monastery once stood.

Opposite: Informatics Centre – a 'computer cathedral' at the University of Sunderland's St Peter's Campus.

ST PETER'S CAMPUS

chapter two

Highlights from History

Part of a prehistoric sand dune can be seen at Claxheugh Rock, South Hylton, which is rich in fossils more than 200 million years old.

CLAXHEUGH ROCK

Fascinating evidence of prehistoric times can be found in Wearside's landscape in unique rock formations, great denes, barrier reef and plants descended from the lush vegetation which once flourished here.

Sunderland is one of the best areas in the world to study the Permian period which was between 280 million and 235 million years ago. It was at this time that a most amazing thing happened where Hetton is now. Long before birds took to their wings, a reptile began to fly. It is the first evidence of a flying vertebrate and we have one of the best fossils ever found of it. The fossil came from Eppleton Quarry, where it probably fell in the water and died, and people come from all over the world to see the Hetton Gliding Reptile in its case at Sunderland Museum.

It was at this time that our unique cannonball rocks were formed. There was open sea to the east of a barrier reef which stretched from South Shields to Teesside, broadly corresponding with today's coastline, and there was a tropical lagoon behind it. As the sea dried up and returned at least five times, cannonball limestone formed at Seaburn, Roker and Fulwell Quarry. The formation, with soft dolomite in the crevices between the cannonball patterns, is found nowhere else in the world.

Humbledon and Tunstall Hills were part of the barrier reef and contain fossils which are 240 million years old. At one point as the huge sea basin dried up, we were in the middle of a desert and part of a dune can still be seen at Claxheugh Rock, South Hylton, where from grazes on the grains of sand, scientists have been able to tell it was very hot, very dry, and that the wind was blowing at 65mph. Claxheugh is also rich in fossils of the Permian period.

The first fossils to be seen in the Sunderland area, however, come from the coal measures dating even earlier, to 300 million years ago. This was a time when Wearside was part of a huge tropical river delta and the land mass that is Britain was migrating slowly northwards. It was a time of giant amphibians, huge freshwater sharks, and plants many times bigger than their descendants – the mare's tail or horsetail plants we see at Whitburn today were then 40 metres high. This lush vegetation decayed and changed into peat which was crushed into coal.

Millions of years later, in the Ice Age, huge glaciers scoured the rocks, effectively obliterating records of the life that went before. The denes – Ryhope, Seaburn, Burdon, Hawthorn, Castle Eden – were gouged out of the coastline. The huge lake behind the coastal reef is known to scientists as Glacial Lake Wear and the River Wear was formed from one of its channels.

The denes of Wearside were gouged out by the huge glaciers of the Ice Age.

Opposite: Hetton Gliding Reptile which took flight more than 200 million years ago.

BURDON DENE

The earliest evidence of human life here can be found in Whitburn Bay after heavy tidal storms. Here, open woodland developed after the last great ice sheet of the Ice Age slowly melted and retreated north, depositing boulder clay over glaciated limestone on cliffs and rocks at Roker, and leaving in its wake raised beaches and shelves still evident today.

Early man hunted in this wilderness. Fragments of Stone Age tools and arrow heads, trees, insects and animals have been found on the beach when the submerged forest has become exposed. People became hunter-gatherers leading a nomadic life, following herds of wild horses and deer to upper Weardale in summer and retreating to the coast in winter, setting up camps in leather tents.

In the New Stone Age (4000 - 1800 BC) people began settling in defined territories, taming animals and growing crops such as corn and cereal, producing pottery and building ceremonial monuments, the first being burial mounds. Good examples can be found at Hasting Hill and Warden Law.

Later, in the Bronze Age (1800 - 800 BC) people began to fashion bronze tools and weapons, examples of which have been found in the river. They made burial mounds, but later began to cremate the dead, making pottery urns for their remains.

Life was good – until a volcanic explosion around 1200 BC changed the climate. And we are still in the climatic Atlantic period today. Archaeological records are very thin from around 1000 BC to the first years AD in this area, but we know that our Iron Age forebears made ditched enclosures, involving considerable community effort, and were farmers – for this is what the Romans found when they arrived.

The extent of Roman occupation of Wearside is a subject of controversy. Some archaeologists believe there was a fort under Sunderland city centre and a dam at Hylton. Others say there is insufficient evidence, although the Victorians certainly removed stones from a structure in the river, re-using them in building the North Pier, and similar cut stones can be seen in the Saxon arch in St Peter's Church.

Local people would have been Romanised during four centuries of occupation, with inter-marriage, and retired Roman soldiers being given land on which to farm. The proximity of Arbeia at South Shields, first fort and then supply base, meant many of the good things in life, like fruit and wine from the Mediterranean, were readily available.

In 410 AD, with the Roman Empire under threat from barbarians, reinforcements from Rome ceased and their administration collapsed. Warlords, then Saxon rulers, took over. Civilisation did not return until the monks arrived in the seventh century.

Whitburn Bay on a winter's day. At times of exceptional tides, remnants of a prehistoric forest and the earliest evidence of human life here are exposed.

Opposite: Seven Sisters (one tree perished) on top of the Stone Age burial mound at Copt Hill.

WHITBURN BAY

Traditionally, Sunderland has been regarded as of historical importance during only two key periods – the golden age of Wearmouth in the seventh century and the industrial revolution in the 19th century. But an archaeological dig under land cleared as part of the regeneration of the south bank of the Wear in the 1990s found evidence indicating Sunderland had extensive trade links with Europe and was of far greater importance in the 16th and 17th centuries than has hitherto been recognised.

Among fragments recovered are about 30 kilogrammes of pottery and a host of clay pipes, dating back to Tudor times and originating across the North Sea. There was evidence of Sunderland's earliest industries. Ships were needed for trading, and timber fragments were found from the rudimentary "raffyards", the earliest shipyards. Panns Bank is so named because of the pans for the salt industry. Six tons of sea water was needed to make one ton of salt, and coal was needed for fuel, but because low-grade coal was adequate for this, higher-grade coal coming down river began to be exported.

The port played an important part in the Civil War, when Sunderland, on the Parliamentary side, was garrisoned and 21,000 Scots soldiers outnumbered the population by ten to one. Coal was supplied to Roundhead London while Royalist Newcastle was closed to the trade, and the coal trade was to remain a mainstay well into the 20th century. The coastal borough of Sunderland had been founded by Norman bishop Hugh du Puiset, and, along with local villages like High Southwick, Newbottle and Tunstall, laid out on regular lines with a long street running east to west. By the end of the 17th century, Sunderland was a busy centre of commerce and industry, with a fine High Street lined with inns and merchants' houses, and its growth outstripped the two parishes of Monkwearmouth and Bishop-wearmouth, to which it then belonged.

The leading men of Sunderland successfully petitioned for a church and parish of their own, fulfilled by an Act of Parliament in 1719 – when the building of Holy Trinity on fine Georgian lines, with square tower, large plain glass windows, grand chancel arch and Corinthian columns, was almost complete.

The Act made the "gentlemen of the vestry" responsible for administering the new parish, so before the Municipal Reform Act of 1835 – when Sunderland had grown important enough to give its name to the new borough – the vestry was the seat of local government. The 24 vestrymen, under the Rector as chairman, debated local affairs, organised social welfare and raised rates, sitting round the huge oak table which is still there.

Lower High Street, showing the Exchange and the Eagle inn.
This was the commercial heart of the old Sunderland.

Opposite: Holy Trinity's Georgian tower is a fine landmark.

LOWER HIGH STREET

The churches of Sunderland and the synagogue in Ryhope Road, are key landmarks not only because of the way their towers grace our skyline, but also because they are the stories in stones of the very different people who were vital players in the making of the modern city.

At one time there were two synagogues, one serving descendants of prosperous Jewish merchants who arrived from western Europe in the 18th century and the other for more traditional Jews whose families arrived as poor refugees from the 19th century pogroms in eastern Europe. Their contribution to business and commerce, the law, medicine and civic life far outweighs their small numbers.

Many Anglican and Methodist churches are testaments to the success of the Victorian industrialists who were their benefactors. By the 19th century, successful businessmen no longer wanted to live in the dirty, overcrowded East End. The rich and successful moved to leafy Ashbrooke, building mansions and lofty churches like Christ Church and St John's Methodist. They also helped build churches for their workers – St Mark's near the glassworks at Millfield, Gothic sandstone St Ignatius at Hendon, and St Columba's red-brick Byzantine basilica at Southwick.

Different groups of newcomers wanted places of worship where they could retain their cultural identity. The Scots, mainly middle-class professionals, built fine Presbyterian churches like St George's. The Irish, mainly labourers fleeing the potato famine at home, were able to practise the Roman Catholicism of their homeland in St Mary's, architect Ignatius Bonomi's early Gothic church built by local Catholics in 1835. Later Italian Redemptorists founded St Benet's.

The churches thrived on the common bonds of their congregations and became lively centres of social life. Often the styles in which they were built tell us a great deal about the kind of people who were their founding congregations. Take Methodism in all its variety – the soaring spires of the Wesleyan churches, looking back to Anglican roots, the galleried preaching houses of the radical Primitives, and the little cottage churches of the fiercely democratic Independents with no paid ministry.

Two churches, St Peter's Monkwearmouth and St Andrew's Roker, rank of national architectural importance. Designed by Edward Prior and with internal features by William Morris and Burne-Jones, St Andrew's has been dubbed "the Cathedral of the Arts and Crafts Movement". And now their surroundings are cleared of the 19th century clutter of little terraces, we can once again appreciate the beautiful lines of St Peter's and St Michael and All Angels, now Sunderland Minster.

Interior view of St Andrew's Church, commonly known as 'the Cathedral of the Arts and Crafts Movement'.

Opposite: Leafy Ashbrooke built by the confident Victorians.

ST ANDREW'S CHURCH

chapter three

The Story of a River

This view of Sunderland Harbour from the sea was painted by the famous artist J.W. Carmichael.

SUNDERLAND HARBOUR

Sunderland was a 19th century tourist attraction, one of the places on a new kind of Grand Tour. Here people could experience two of the wonders of the modern industrial world – if they had the stomach, that is.

Here they found the longest single-span iron bridge in the world and the deepest coal mine, down which visitors' trips, in an open bucket, were on offer. One visitor recorded his impressions of the trip down Wearmouth Colliery on the north bank of the river and the terror of stepping into the iron bucket "swinging over the black depth of 1,800 feet, with nothing between its bottom and the bottom of the shaft." He wrote: "You look round for refuge and your eyes are filled with coal dust... you would lay hold of a post to keep up your courage but there is not one; you look down to the ground to avoid ugly objects, and lo! the pit mouth yawns beneath your feet..."

Crossing the bridge had its terrors too. A French traveller, Louis Simond, recorded his impressions in a journal of his tour of Britain in 1810 and 1811, published in Edinburgh in 1815. He recorded that the Sunderland bridge "is certainly a wonderful object, for its lightness and boldness. Vessels with masts 100 feet high can pass under it. The wind blew today in a perfect hurricane and when we crossed the bridge it was really terrifying."

The bridge even attracted a Swedish industrial spy, Eric Svedenstierna, who reported: "This is the largest and finest iron bridge which has yet been built anywhere. It is 236 English feet long between the two ends of the arch and so high that three-masted vessels can sail away under it with full sail. Everywhere in England one comes across engraved drawings, views and descriptions of this bridge and at the inn where I stopped at mid-day the bills were embellished with an engraved view of it."

The bridge was completed in 1796 and was a remarkable feat in its day. It was only the second iron bridge ever to be built, the first being the much smaller one at Coalbrookdale. To build an iron bridge of this size required a great leap of faith on the part of its sponsor, Rowland Burdon MP, and great skill from its Sunderland engineer, Tommy Wilson.

A grand procession preceded the great pomp of the opening ceremony, presided over by Prince William of Gloucester and attended by 80,000 people. The new bridge gave direct access between Monkwearmouth and Bishopwearmouth, previously linked only by ferries. Until then, development had been along the line of the river, with its coal trade, shipyards and associated industries. Roads spread from the bridge to north and south. The shape of Sunderland was to change forever.

The first Wearmouth Bridge was the longest single-span cast iron bridge in the world and was one of the wonders of the industrial age. This aquatint by J. Radfield in 1798 shows the west view.

Opposite: Sunset over Wearmouth Bridge which replaced the cast iron bridge on the same site.

CAST IRON BRIDGE

The river had always been the lifeblood of the communities along its banks, but its transformation into a great industrial highway was largely due to the work of the River Wear Commissioners. Industries were able to thrive along the banks due to great feats of engineering in the river itself.

The Commissioners, formed in 1717, built piers and lighthouses, imposed regulation on the overcrowded river, dredged it, and transformed it into a deeper and narrower channel.

They commissioned works of art, including portraits of themselves and prominent shipowners and more importantly, major events in the development of the port. Two of the greatest Victorian achievements were the creation of the South Docks and the opening of the south outlet direct to the sea, and both are captured in several paintings. Those by James Wilson Carmichael and Mark Thompson, in particular, show how local people turned out in force to celebrate these great events. These and other treasures were handed over to Sunderland Museum after the last meeting of the RWC in 1973, when their function was taken over by the Port of Sunderland Authority.

The 18th century saw the building of magnificent piers, lighthouses and quays, but, recorded historian W.C. Mitchell, "more wonderful than these monuments of skills and industry is the great change which has taken place in the river".

He recorded that "enormous rocks and sandbanks have been removed; land has been reclaimed on both banks, it has been widened in places and thousands of tons of river substance have been dredged from its bed, so that vessels of the largest size may enter or leave the port at any period of the tide".

Storms took their toll. The South Pier had to be rebuilt in a less exposed direction after damage during a violent storm which wrecked 34 ships at the mouth of the Wear in 1771.

And in 1836 a winter storm wreaked havoc in the harbour, including damage to the old South Pier lighthouse, which, like the Eddystone, was made of wood. It was replaced in 1856 by a higher structure which served more than a century and is now preserved on Cliffe Park.

Then there was the spectacular removal en bloc of the old North Pier lighthouse in 1841. After a breach by the sea, the pier was substantially rebuilt, lengthened and strengthened, and the channel to sea straightened and deepened. Then wheels and bars were inserted underneath and the entire octagonal lighthouse in polished stone weighing 338 tons, was moved in a cradle, at the rate of one or two feet a minute, for a distance of 450 feet. The foundations were then rebuilt. It was another remarkable feat of engineering for the Wear.

A painting of the opening of the South Docks in 1850, by J.W. Carmichael.

Opposite: Sunrise over Roker Pier.

OPENING OF THE SOUTH DOCKS

First shipbuilding town in the world – that was Sunderland's claim by the 19th century. A host of subsidiary industries, including forges, anchor-makers, ropeworks, sailmakers, and later sheetmetal works, and many others, sprang up. The river was booming.

Potteries, bottleworks and glassworks grew up on the back of the coal trade as colliers returning to the Wear brought back as ballast the fine sand and other materials they needed. Then they spotted a lucrative new market in souvenirs of Sunderland, which were sent by ship all over the world. Local people, proud of their burgeoning town, also bought them in huge numbers. The most popular image was the iron bridge, new buildings were also featured, and there was usually a verse too. There are many fine examples in the glass and pottery collection at Sunderland Museum.

But shipbuilding and coal were the bedrock of the town. As William Fordyce reported in his History and Antiquities of the County Palatine of Durham (1857): "From the entrance of the harbour up to Hylton Ferry the banks of the Wear on both sides are crowded with shipbuilding yards, docks etc, presenting in a most striking point of view an exemplification of the enterprise and industry which have effectively conduced to the propriety of the port.

"Scarcely an opening on the shore of the river or a nook or crevice in the limestone rocks which overhang it can be found in which a ship of large and small dimensions is not in the course of erection. Sunderland is emphatically the first shipbuilding port in the world."

At the time, Sunderland was rated the fourth port in Britain in terms of the aggregate tonnage. The shipment of coal, the principal business, amounted to 1,300,000 tons a year. But the east coast coal route was the most notorious for wrecks.

Although we think of the economy as being dominated by heavy industry, the largest single occupation in Sunderland was seafaring; one in four men aged over 20 went to sea in 1861. This was the most hazardous occupation of all. The losses were astounding. In 1881, one in every 56 British seamen, 4,000 in all, perished at sea. The first seamen's union was started by a Sunderland man, Joseph Havelock Wilson.

The weather was often blamed, but half the 20,000 coastal wrecks in the decade up to 1875 went down in only a strong breeze. Campaigner Samuel Plimsoll found overloading and undermanning, bad storage, bad design, defective construction and lack of repair. Nor did owners lose out; ships were frequently over-insured, and earned the local nickname "coffin ships". Widows without means had to send their sons to the local Boys' Orphanage to train for the sea.

This painting by Thomas Hemy shows the hive of industry on the banks of the River Wear in 1882.

Opposite: 19th century advert for shipbuilders, Bartram and Sons.

RIVER INDUSTRY

As sail gave way to steam and wood to metal, the many tiny shipbuilding outfits on the Wear – often two shipwrights and an apprentice building on any tiny stretch of river they could find – closed one by one. The depressions of the 1840s and 1880s also took their toll, so by the 20th century, only the big names, famous the world over, were left.

By the time of the Great War, 16 yards were left to meet the increased demand for ships. Of these, Bartram's, which launched directly into the sea from the yard in the South Dock; Sir James Laing, Short Brothers, J.L. Thompson, Crown's, S.P. Austin, William Pickersgill, and William Doxford, all survived to make a vital contribution in the Second World War. Doxford's was also the greatest of all the great names in marine engineering on the Wear. Before the Second World War, the Doxford engine, built both here and elsewhere under licence, had a 90 per cent share of the world market.

Both wars saw the yards working flat out, but peacetime brought fluctuating fortunes. Shipbuilding drifted along in the post-war years, and despite some contraction, there were still 30,000 shipbuilding and engineering workers on the Wear in the 1960s. The Geddes Report of 1966 prepared the way for major restructuring but by then Austin and Pickersgill were already merged, soon to be joined by Bartram's, and Doxford, Laing and Thompson's were also linked. Shipbuilding continued to go through its inevitable peaks and troughs, although orders on the Wear never really dried up, with A and P's highly successful SD14 programme of 14,000-tonners providing plenty of work and berths at Pallion, Deptford and North Sands also remaining busy.

Major upheavals came with high-flying Court Line taking over the Doxford group – only months before it collapsed. Labour Minister Tony Benn stepped in and the Government took the yards over, a precursor to nationalisation of the entire shipbuilding industry in 1977, but Bartram's closed in 1978, followed by North Sands and Deptford in the 1980s.

A and P and Sunderland Shipbuilders, both with covered-in facilities which were the most modern in Europe, joined to form North East Shipbuilders in 1986. Following contractual difficulties over an order for Danish ferries, the partnership was wound up in 1989 with operating losses in their millions. The community united in a highly emotive campaign to save the yards, but to no avail. A tradition which had produced magnificent vessels from the Torrens, the elegant full-rigged passenger clipper whose speed broke records on the Australia run, to the mighty 65,000-ton Borgsten, was brought to an end.

These Danish ferries were the last ships to be built on the Wear before the shipyards closed in 1989.

Opposite: A barrage balloon flying over a busy wartime river scene.

LAST SHIPS

The River Wear is silent now, save for the song of birds no longer drowned out by the clang of metal on metal. Gulls, terns and kittiwakes gather at the river mouth, while at low tide wading birds, including redshank, curlew and dunlin, feed on the exposed mud along the whole length of the river. Tourism and leisure have taken over from heavy industry.

Now the ten-mile stretch of river from Fatfield, at the heart of the Great North Forest, to the sea, is linked to a network of paths, cycle tracks and bridleways. These provide short circular walks as well as links to longer distance routes like the Weardale Way or the cycle route all the way from our coast to the sea at Whitehaven in Cumbria.

Yet once, even in an apparently rural backwater like South Hylton, there were great potteries, and here was the site of the ferry for coaches and horses on the main route to Newcastle before the building of the iron bridge in 1796. A coble ferry also took men to and from work at Hylton Colliery, Castletown.

The 12 arches of the Victoria Viaduct, over which steam trains once puffed on the old main rail line to London, still stride across the river at Sir James Steel Park near Fatfield. The bridge, which opened on Queen Victoria's Coronation Day in 1838, is modelled on a Roman bridge at Alcantara in Spain. So we have a mock Roman bridge within view from a mock Greek temple at Penshaw Monument (see page 61).

At Cox Green the remains of two slipways from three old boat-building yards, can still be seen. Look out too for Alice's Well, which used to be Cox Green's only source of fresh water until after the Second World War.

On the north side, the riverside trail also takes in the Wildfowl and Wetlands Trust at Washington, home to 1,200 swans, geese, ducks and a magnificent flock of pink flamingos.

Oak and ash woodlands have cloaked the banks of the Wear since the last Ice Age and walking through them today, you may spot the woodpecker, flycatcher and sparrowhawk in the trees towering above, while at their feet you can see woodland wild flowers such as bluebell, wood sorrel and wild garlic.

Further east, there is Claxheugh Rock, a limestone and sandstone cliff over 200 million years old, rich in fossils and home to rare plants such as rock rose, fairy flax and blue moor grass.

On the opposite bank, nearer the sea, Timber Beach nature reserve, which owes its name to the days when timber for building wooden ships was stored there, is an important saltmarsh. Plants include sea aster and glasswort. Above the saltmarsh, wonderful wild flower meadows harbour adder's tongue fern, wild angelica and other rare species.

Washington Staithes, now a rural backwater, opposite Cox Green.

Opposite: Victoria Viaduct was based on the Roman bridge at Alcantara in Spain and was opened in 1838 on the day of Queen Victoria's Coronation.

WASHINGTON STAITHES

The stretch of river from Queen Alexandra Bridge to the sea was the hub of Sunderland industry almost to the end of the 20th century. The bridge now looks down over a very different scene.

Here twin giants, Austin and Pickersgill and the old Doxford shipyard faced one another across the river. The Southwick plant has vanished under the Enterprise Park which stretches along the hinterland to the A19, but ship-related work continues at the Pallion yard.

Below the bridge, Webster's Ropery, dating from 1793, was the first of the great old riverside buildings to be restored. Now there are others presenting a fine frontage around the new Fish Quay, looking across to the National Glass Centre, St Peter's Campus of the University of Sunderland, North Sands Business Centre and the new housing development which sweeps over former industrial land right down to the marina where the North Dock used to be.

From Wearmouth Bridge, the north bank is adorned by sculptures expressing Wearside's past and present and hopes for its future. Artists worked with local people who contributed ideas and who sometimes had a practical input too. Old craftsmen advised artists on how to achieve certain effects, as with the brilliant piece of metalworking skill in which old industrial girders split to form into a cormorant poised for flight. The Red House, lifesize ruins in sandstone reclaimed from Queen Alexandra Bridge, stands where a crane once towered over J. L. Thompson's shipyard and depicts how people once lived.

At Look Out Hill where Wearsiders waited for the first sight of a ship with a loved one aboard, there is a stone picnic basket, blanket and a telescope. All along the riverside walk, stone rivets remind us of the industrial past and near Wearmouth Bridge, a shadow from a different time falls as a geometric pattern in the pavement is transformed into a hammerhead crane when viewed through a telescope. This stands at the foot of a giant metal tree whose base is a five-metre concrete block once used for mooring ships. The steel tree weighs six tons and towers 30 feet above the riverside, its roots in the past and its branches stretching symbolically into the future.

Ambit, the newest piece of public art in the city, is believed to be one of the largest pieces of waterborne art in the world. Its 24 stainless steel tubes are linked and anchored to the riverbed on the site of Austin's Pontoon where ships were raised and lowered to the Wear. By day it resembles a boom, but by night it shimmers into light beneath the bridge.

This giant metal tree, roots in the past in a concrete block once used for mooring ships, and branches reaching to the future, is part of the riverside sculpture trail.

Opposite: A cormorant poised for flight, formed from old industrial girders.

TREE SCULPTURE

chapter four

From Black to Green

Idyllic woodland in the midst of the old coalfield area at Hetton.

HIGH HOUSES WOOD

Wildlife flourishes where wagonways once wound their way from collieries to staithes by the river and pulley wheels have been replaced by trees on the skyline. Everywhere the black of the coal industry has given way to green around old pit villages which are now part of the City of Sunderland – and which played such a crucial role in the growth of Wearside. For the pit heaps which have gone were both blots on the landscape and symbols of prosperity built on coal and on the backbreaking labour of the miners.

Hetton Lyons Park, with its ponds, meadows and woodland, now stands on the site of the old Hetton Colliery – literally a groundbreaking venture – for it was the first to break through the layer of magnesian limestone covering the coal reserves. To the west of Hetton and Houghton, where the coal was nearer the surface and more easily won, many smaller pits sprang up over the years, sending their coals by keelboats down the river for loading on to ships. To the east there were no pits at all until the risky venture undertaken by the Hetton Coal Company in 1820.

When the coal was finally found 19 months after the sinking began, it was so rich that further pits were developed at Elemore and Eppleton. Then came Houghton in 1823 and South Hetton in 1830. Although Wearsiders tend to think of Hetton in terms of 19th century mining, the settlement goes back much further than that. It was an old farming settlement and it is first recorded in the Boldon Book of the 12th century. Its name comes from an old English word meaning "where the dogroses grow".

Now wild flowers are blooming again on the Coalfield Way and along the Stephenson Trail, route of the world's first steam railway.

Winning the coal from the inhospitable ground was not the only pioneering venture at the new Hetton Colliery. The great civil engineers George and Robert Stephenson, more famous for their later work in creating the world's first steam-operated passenger railway from Stockton to Darlington, were called in to solve the problem of transporting coal over the hilly ground to the staithes on the river and on to the sea.

It was here that they gave the world the first railway designed from the outset for steam locomotives. The early locos, using a rope haulage system on the steepest inclines, transported coal direct to Bishopwearmouth, dispensing with the need for the age-old keel-boats.

On September 18, 1822, people came from all over the country to cheer the Puffing Billies on their first journey, and engineers came from Europe and America to see this revolution in land transport.

Where Hetton Colliery once stood, Hetton Lyons Park provides a green oasis, with ponds, meadows and woodland.

HETTON COUNTRY PARK

The story of local miners, whose labour fuelled the Industrial Revolution, is one of courage and comradeship, constant danger, incredible hardship and an indomitable spirit. Their common bond to build a better life led to self-help movements, unions and co-operatives, and a sense of community that survives to this day.

Working "marras" down the pit were much more than colleagues. They were bound by dependence on one another, even for their lives. And there are countless stories of men sacrificing themselves in bids to rescue comrades when disaster struck.

From the start, there were inherent dangers in winning coal – roof collapses, haulage accidents, inundations of water, gas and explosions all took their toll.

Coal had been known in Durham from Roman times, but the Boldon Book of 1183 is among the first documentary evidence. In the 14th century as forests began to be depleted, coal grew in economic importance and mines spread out from the banks of the Wear into the surrounding countryside. By 1600, shafts had been sunk to shallow seams to create "bell" pits, worked only so far as ventilation would allow, and in the 17th and 18th centuries, mechanical pumping and primitive ventilation systems brought further development. By the early 19th century, the new steam power enabled deeper pits to be sunk.

Hetton, as we have seen, was first to break through the magnesian limestone, followed by Eppleton and Elemore, then others including South Hetton, Haswell, Wearmouth, Murton, followed in the 1840s by Seaton and Seaham – where a harbour had been created by Lord Londonderry in 1828 to export coal from Rainton where his wife's family, the Vane Tempests, had workings.

The other main coal-owning family at the time was the Lambtons, who had Lady Ann, Dorothea, Margaret, "D" pit, Herrington, Houghton and Lumley Sixth, and engineering works at Philadelphia.

This empire, crucial to the development of Sunderland, was taken over by James Joicey in 1869. That year, a downturn in trade caused owners to demand savage cuts in piece-rate earnings. At Wearmouth earnings were cut first by 16 per cent, then by 33 per cent, and there was a similar pattern elsewhere. A series of strikes swept the county, rekindling the spirit of trade unionism. The Durham Miners' Association was formed and the condition of child miners, described overleaf, was one of its major concerns.

The 20th century brought nationalisation, competition from other fuels, mechanisation and rationalisation, with closures in the west leading to production centring on big coastal pits. In 1993, Wearmouth Colliery closed. Now the Durham Coalfield is no more.

Miners leave a shift at Eppleton Colliery, one of the first to be sunk following the ground-breaking venture at Hetton.

Opposite: Miner's lamp.

END OF A SHIFT

Still fast asleep, they were carried to work on the backs of their fathers or older brothers through the dark streets to the darker pit in the early hours of the morning. These were the infants working as trapper boys, some only five or six years old, in pits throughout the Durham coalfield.

A 16-hour day was the norm for the lads, who were up at 3am six days a week to go to work, then home to supper and bed. No time to play for them. They kept a lonely vigil, opening and shutting the trap doors on the underground wagonway for older boys, putters who pushed the coal tubs along or drivers who directed the ponies pulling tubs. Often they sat in complete darkness. If they were lucky, their family could afford two candles which they had to try to make last the whole shift.

There had been an outcry over the conditions of child chimney sweeps and conditions for factory lads were governed by Acts of Parliament. But there was no legislation to protect the children of the pits, whose conditions, even by the standards of the 19th century, were horrendous. They were forgotten and even today little has been written about their plight.

The fledgling Pitmen's Union led by Thomas Hepburn of Hetton won a major concession in 1831 for boys to work only 12-hour shifts. But the union was broken and it was back to shifts of 16 hours and more. It was the committee of inquiry into the St Hilda's Colliery explosion of 1839 which discovered "inhuman practices" in the work of infants underground and called for a Royal Commission. This led to the age of entry to the pits being raised to ten years. By 1872, boys' hours were ten per day plus 20 hours' schooling a fortnight. The Commission's inspector John Roby Leifchild had been horrified by what he found. He discovered not only the 16-hour norm, but also children who were left down the pit 24, 36 and 48 hours – and one who was underground for an entire week.

Infants made up one fifth of the workforce in Wearside pits. Families had little choice – they needed the coppers children could earn and when work was short, the man with sons would be taken on first, for children were cheap and could save a man's wages for the owner. There again, families lived in tied pit houses, so if a father was killed, his family was evicted – unless his children were miners.

Leifchild found one such breadwinner down Wearmouth pit. He was seven years old and had been at work in the pit the day his father was killed by an explosion. The memory still troubled him. He told the inspector he felt the blast "like a heavy wind and it blew all the candles out..."

First day at Wearmouth Colliery for Tim Hopper and Arthur Youern, both aged 14, in 1919. But in the 19th century children as young as five or six went down the pit.

Opposite: Pulley wheels used to dominate the skyline.

CHILD MINERS

It is fitting that two pieces of mining heritage, the Washington 'F' pithead buildings and the Bowes Railway, survive in Washington, for the old pit villages in the new township are steeped in mining history. At the beginning of the 19th century, 23 collieries teemed their coals into keels on a two-mile stretch from Lambton Park to Washington Staithes, and 300 keels passed down to Sunderland each tide to load up seagoing colliers.

The first steam engine ever used for draining coal mines was built by Thomas Newcomen in 1718 on Washington Moor, where coal was worked as early as 1356.

Nearby Biddick Colliery clocked up four "firsts" – in 1732 , an attempt to produce artificial ventilation by means of a furnace at the bottom of a shaft; in 1753, coal was raised to the surface by steam power; in 1750 it had a furnace on the surface to draw up foul air from the shaft; and in 1763 it was the first in the Durham coalfield to use the flint-and-steel mill for safer lighting.

The Washington 'F' pit has a remarkable history. It was the sixth pit, all named after letters of the alphabet, on the site in 1777 and was sunk to a depth of 929 feet, becoming one of the earliest working deep pits in the country. It closed after flooding due to an explosion in 1796 but reopened 25 years later. In 1856 the shaft was deepened to more than 200 metres and by 1870 it was the major coal producer in the area. The pit, which employed 1,500 men, was producing half a million tons of saleable coal when it closed in 1968.

The pithead, with its headgear, winding house and the only steam winding engine still in its original location in the Durham coalfield, gained recognition from English Heritage in 1999 and has Grade II listed status.

The twin cylinder horizontal steam engine was made in 1888 and a short film recorded before closure shows it working under steam.

When it closed its pit heap was 200 feet high and contained 1.63 million tons of waste. Some of this was converted to red shale and used in the construction of roads and the remainder forms the basis of Albany Park in Washington.

George Stephenson was called in to be engineer of the railway, later to become known as the Bowes Railway, at Springwell Colliery in 1826, though it is likely that Stephenson's pupil Joseph Locke was resident engineer. The site has the only preserved standard gauge rope haulage system in the world.

The Bowes Railway Museum underwent a £100,000 restoration in 1999, thanks to grants from Europe and the National Lottery, and was chosen to host a Millennium Festival of Railway Heritage. A train pulled by a steam engine operates on special days to the delight of local children.

Washington 'F' pit was one of the earliest working deep pits in the country in 1777.

Opposite: Open day for children at Bowes Railway.

WASHINGTON 'F' PIT

Silksworth is the only pit heap still to dominate the Sunderland skyline, in its role as our only ski slope, part of a sports and leisure complex. Another sports landmark on an old colliery site is Sunderland AFC's Stadium of Light, where "superpit" Wearmouth stood for 170 years.

To the west of the city, where pits closed first, there is green and pleasant land. It is 50 years since Hetton closed. Now shy grey-necked herons fish in Lyons Lake in the early morning. Later wildfowl and watersports enthusiasts may appear. Nearby Blossom Pond, fringed by bulrushes and great willowherb, is a haunt of wetland birds.

Heritage trails devised by the city's countryside team also direct us to times past. They take us past Hetton's vast Primitive Methodist Chapel, built in the mid-19th century by miners themselves as a successor to the smaller chapel founded by their early leader, Thomas Hepburn, and a testament to the role Methodism played in educating and helping miners improve their lives.

From here we move to Copt Hill, topped by a line of trees known as the Seven Sisters (though there are only six left - see page 24) said to watch over ancient remains, some dating from 4000 BC, in the barrow beneath.

Wearside's highest point at Warden Law enjoys magnificent views. Here horses once had to help steam engines on Stephenson's early railway, while on the way down the speed of the wagons had to be controlled by a haulage rope with a brake attached.

A two-mile loop in the trail between Rainton Bridge and East Rainton takes in Joe's Pond, an attractive wetland. It is named after Joe Wilson, a pit sawyer who leased the pond from the National Coal Board in the 1950s and single-handedly created an important habitat for wildlife.

Dug in the mid-19th century to provide clay for making bricks, the pond later had a new industrial use supplying water for engines at Nicholson Colliery. Joe Wilson stocked it with plants and fish and built islands for birds to nest. The pond, now managed by Durham Wildlife Trust, is nationally recognised as a Site of Special Scientific Importance.

Massive reclamation has transformed Rye Hill, adjacent to Joe's Pond. RJB Mining, in partnership with the City of Sunderland Council, transplanted ancient hedgerows and woodland to the periphery before recovering 829,000 tonnes of quality coal from it. Even when the site resembled a lunar landscape, wildlife began to arrive. Now it is Rainton Meadows prime nature reserve.

And at Herrington, 100 years of waste was accumulated in a sprawling heap of 10 million tonnes. RJB's coal recovery project set the target completion date at the Millennium and in the early years of the 21st century a country park will develop.

Joe's Pond is named after a pit sawyer who single-handedly created an important habitat for wildlife from an old industrial pond.

Opposite: The black of the coal industry has given way to green around old pit villages where wild flowers are blooming again.

JOE'S POND

chapter five

Landmarks Then and Now

The Wearmouth Bridge, designed by Mott, Hay & Anderson was constructed in 1929. The original bridge, erected in 1796, was the largest iron bridge in the world and a technological wonder of its day.

WEARMOUTH BRIDGE

Sunderland Yacht Club's superb new clubhouse, costing £750,000, opened in 1998. It replaced the old clubhouse, which stood on land needed for the impressive marina housing development. With its outstanding facilities and spectacular sea views, Sunderland Yacht Club, along with Sunderland Marina and the Marine Activities Centre, is putting Sunderland on the map as a first class sailing venue. Major televised competitions such as the Ultra 30 and UK 18ft Skiff Grand Prix have been attracted to Sunderland bringing Olympic and World class competitors to experience the thrill of North Sea sailing off Roker.

SUNDERLAND YACHT CLUB

Washington Old Hall is medieval in origin and is the ancestral home of George Washington's family. Because of this link, it is a favourite calling point for American visitors and the raising of the Stars and Stripes is an annual ceremony around American Independence Day. Extensively rebuilt in the 17th century, the hall retained original details like 12th century stone arches. A Grade I listed building, it is preserved by the National Trust as a fine example of a 17th century manor house with a collection of delftware, oil paintings and richly carved oak furniture.

WASHINGTON OLD HALL

The stylish UK Headquarters and European Financial Support Centre of Nike (UK) Ltd is located at Doxford International – the UK's most successful Enterprise Zone Business Park, and the heart of the city's thriving customer and financial service industry. Doxford International has been successfully developed over the past eight years by Akeler in partnership with the City of Sunderland.

NIKE

Penshaw Monument is Sunderland's most prominent landmark. Visible for miles around, it stands on Penshaw Hill round which the legendary Lambton Worm was supposed to wind itself ten times. Modelled on the Greek Temple of Theseion, it was erected by public subscription in memory of John George Lambton, 1st Earl of Durham, otherwise known as Radical Jack. He campaigned for parliamentary reform in 1832, his report on Canada is said to be the foundation of the Commonwealth of Nations, and he promoted accident insurance and a pension scheme for miners in his pits, who were free to join unions.

PENSHAW MONUMENT

Hylton Castle was built around 1400 by William de Hylton in the shape of an enormous gatehouse designed for comfort rather than defence. Excavations in the 1990s found evidence of a much larger baronial settlement, indicating that the Hylton family were of greater significance through medieval and Elizabethan times than previously thought. The family survived a scandal, when Sir Robert Hylton killed a stable lad called Roger Skelton with a scythe. The baron was granted a free pardon in 1609, but the ghost of "the Cauld Lad of Hylton" is said to haunt the castle to this day.

HYLTON CASTLE

The magnificent Stadium of Light is one of Sunderland's newest landmarks. Standing majestically on the banks of the Wear, the stadium replaced much-loved Roker Park as the home of Sunderland AFC, providing state-of-the-art accommodation for players and supporters alike. Its bowl-like design helps make the famous roar, which has inspired the Lads for generations, reverberate around the ground. Built on the site of Wearmouth Colliery, once the deepest coal mine in the world, it heralds dynamic revitalisation of surrounding brownfield land.

STADIUM OF LIGHT

Sunderland Empire is the largest theatre in the North East and the major venue for live entertainment in the city. Designed by the local Milburn brothers, it is a fine example of Edwardian theatre architecture and is one of the few survivors of the great Moss Empires chain. It was opened in 1907 by Vesta Tilley, one of the major stars of the day, who made her name as a male impersonator. It fell on hard times in the 1950s, but was taken over by Sunderland Council in 1959.

THE SUNDERLAND EMPIRE

The Pinewood Building at the City of Sunderland College's Hylton Centre which specialises in training for the leisure industry. It incorporates a restaurant and bistro, hairdressing and beauty salon and travel agent's, all of which are open to members of the public – who can also join the leisure club, where facilities include swimming pool, sauna, steam room and gymnasium.

CITY OF SUNDERLAND COLLEGE

Fulwell Mill is the most complete windmill in the North East. It was built as a tower mill of magnesian limestone from nearby quarries once worked by the Romans. Although there are records showing it was built for Sunderland shipowner Matthew Robson Swan in 1821, a 1785 map shows that an earlier mill stood on the site. A £700,000 restoration, including grants from the European Regional Development Fund and National Lottery Heritage Fund, will create a living museum and the mill will once more be capable of producing organic flour and bread.

FULWELL MILL

The Solar Office at Doxford International Business Park is the most environmentally advanced office building in Europe. With one of the world's largest integrated photovoltaic façades, the 38,764 sq.ft. building is designed to be both energy producing and energy saving.

SOLAR OFFICE

chapter six

Preserving the Past for the Future

The old South Pier lighthouse was moved from its original location to Cliffe Park where it is preserved for all to see.

OLD SOUTH PIER LIGHTHOUSE

Sunderland has a proud history of preserving the past for the benefit of future generations, and indeed in 1846, was the first place outside London to have a publicly funded museum. It was popular with Wearsiders from the start, visitor figures have grown year on year, and in the 1990s our museums won "premier league" status from the Government because of the importance of the industrial, art and natural sciences collections. A shipyard gallery and a coal gallery were designed to reconstruct the sights and sounds of shipbuilding and mining in Sunderland Museum and Art Gallery, where the collection also includes important exhibits from the glass and pottery industries, while Monkwearmouth Station Museum is a listed building in its own right.

The museum's first home was in the Athenaeum in Fawcett Street in 1846 and it took over the private collections, mainly of natural history items, built up from 1836 by the Sunderland Natural History and Antiquarian Society. It was joined by the new public library in 1858. Together they moved to the present museum building in 1879, and remained inextricably linked, until the library moved out to new premises in Fawcett Street in 1995 providing more space, particularly for its busy local studies section, which houses important documents from our heritage.

Sunderland Museum itself is one of the city's oldest and grandest public buildings. It was designed by J. and T. Tillman in their own version of French chateau style and built by W. D. Allison, the Whitburn builder whose other outstanding work includes St Andrew's Church, Roker. The building incorporated the library and art gallery plus Winter Gardens which housed exotic plants, talking parrots and other birds.

The ceremony for the laying of the foundation stone, by the Mayor, Alderman Samuel Storey, was attended by former U.S. President Ulysses S. Grant, and some of the most eminent men of letters of the day took an interest in the project, largely through Thomas Dixon, a self-educated local cork-cutter and outstanding example of the Victorian passion for self-improvement. John Ruskin, whose Letters to a Working Man, were addressed to Dixon, provided designs for the gallery, Dante Gabriel Rossetti was persuaded to give paintings of two heads, and French painter Alphone Legros painted a portrait of Dixon in front of an audience on the opening day.

As early as 1896 there were plans for an extension, but it was not until 1964 that a new block was built on the site of the Winter Gardens which were hit during a bombing raid in 1941. Now a remodelled museum will be linked to new Winter Gardens in an exciting scheme outlined in our final chapter.

Sunderland Museum, with the Winter Gardens, seen from across the lake in Mowbray Park in the 1930s.

Opposite: The grand entrance to Sunderland Museum from Borough Road.

SUNDERLAND MUSEUM

The building itself is undoubtedly the finest exhibit in the collection at Monkwearmouth Station Museum. Its classical stone façade, with Ionic pillars and portico, make it one of Sunderland's grandest landmarks. It is also a fitting monument to the importance of Sunderland in the development of the railways.

Yet its future hung in the balance at the beginning of the 1970s after the last passengers alighted. It was saved for posterity when the council bought it from British Rail for just £4,000 in 1971. Two years later, after considerable renovation, it reopened as the first station in the country to be converted into a museum. The museum has won several awards, the latest, at the end of 1999, being national recognition for its work with children – a recent major development has been of a children's gallery for under eights including a model railway and play train and dressing up clothes for imaginative play.

Stepping inside the museum today, visitors are transported to a Victorian booking hall, much as it looked when the station was built in 1848. Then, it was a grand train terminus for Monkwearmouth, and, before the building of the railway bridge in 1879, passengers travelling to the other side of the river, where there were stations at Hendon and Burdon Road, had to get off the train and either walk or take a horse-drawn cab across the road bridge.

Originally, there was a small station for Monkwearmouth at the Wheatsheaf after the building of the Brandling Junction Railway between Gateshead and Monkwearmouth in 1839. This railway was bought by George Hudson, the "Railway King", who then built the fine new station as a showpiece.

However, its grandeur had less to do with its place in Hudson's York, Newcastle and Berwick Railway (later part of the North Eastern Railway) than with his desire to make a grand gesture following his election in 1845 as Tory MP for Sunderland.

At the time he was at the height of his fame. Later he sank into notoriety – he has been described as the first of the modern big-time financial swindlers – but he survived as MP until 1859, long after his fall from grace. For whatever the truth of his other financial dealings, there is no doubt that Sunderland benefited from huge investment by Hudson, particularly in the docks and railways.

Earlier we described how George Stephenson developed the world's first railway designed for steam power for Hetton Colliery. In George Hudson as our MP, we also had the first person to spot the commercial potential of the railways and the need for a national network which he tried to achieve with a series of amalgamations.

Monkwearmouth Station, built on Greek classical lines in 1848, is one of Sunderland's most important old industrial buildings and is preserved as a popular museum.

Opposite: Election poster for George Hudson who built the Monkwearmouth Station.

MONKWEARMOUTH STATION

A remarkable transformation has taken place on the south bank of the river where some of Sunderland's finest old buildings have been restored.

An 18th century bonded warehouse has been saved by conversion into a students' union bar, retaining the original features including the hoist used for lifting goods from wagons directly to the first floor.

Further down Low Street, the Rose Line building at Wylam Wharf has been redeveloped by local company, Rivergreen Developments plc, and transformed into office accommodation and, fronting on the river, Brasserie 21 one of the best restaurants in the region. A new office building, designed to complement the old, is being built alongside.

And straddling Low Street and High Street, the old Exchange represents perhaps the most remarkable transformation of all. The building opened in 1814 and was right in the heart of the business centre of the parish of Sunderland. Designed in classical style and built in stone with a stucco façade, it was used for cultural and leisure pursuits as well as mercantile activities. It originally had a clock turret – a replica has now been built – and there was an open arcade between two end pavilions. It was built by George Cameron, grandfather of Joseph Swan the inventor.

It was the scene of many grand social events. Best recorded of these was when the Marquess of Londonderry entertained his old commander from the Peninsular War, the Duke of Wellington, and Sir Walter Scott in 1827. Sir Walter recorded the event in his diary, reporting that the Duke was "brilliantly received by an immense population, chiefly seamen". The dinner was followed by a brilliant ball in the Assembly Garth with "the cream of Northern society".

The Exchange was at the heart of a national scandal when merchants tried to cover up Britain's first outbreak of cholera in 1831-32 to prevent Sunderland's trade being interrupted by a naval quarantine. The scandal also highlighted the squalor and public health dangers of the East End and the need for the reform of administration, then handled by the Improvement Commissioners and similar local authorities with specific functions.

And it was in the Exchange – against the wishes of the Commissioners, that the Borough of Sunderland was born in 1836. The Borough Council continued to meet there until 1842.

Until the 1870s, it was the place of Parliamentary hustings and then had diverse uses before falling derelict. In the 1990s, the former Tyne and Wear Development Corporation, with English Heritage support, came to the rescue with a £1million restoration, including the distinctive clock tower, and a successful bid bringing a further £2.7million grant from the National Lottery Heritage Fund. It is to become a prestigious arts venue, with auditorium and restaurant.

Restored buildings on Sunderland's revitalised waterfront including the clock tower of the Exchange, Sunderland's first town hall and the colourful Rose Line building.

Opposite: View of the Exchange from High Street.

ON THE WATERFRONT

Waterworks, whose grandeur symbolises the importance of water to the Victorians, are among our most important industrial monuments today.

Improved water supplies and sanitation proved to be the most significant of all health-improvement measures and played a vital role in curbing cholera, which had spread fast in the slums of the East End with its middens, shared privies and overcrowded conditions.

Water was also vital for the steam power needed by new industries mushrooming along the riverbanks. And, of course, its health-giving properties as an alternative drink to alcohol were extolled by the temperance movement – Mrs Ormistan Chant of the British Women's Temperance League declared Sunderland water was the most delicious she had tasted in ten years of water drinking.

The first water company in Sunderland was Bishopwearmouth, formed in 1824, which raised water from a 49-metre well in Waterworks Road. By 1845, 670 houses out of 6,086 had a water supply – the highest proportion of any town in the North East. But supply was scarce and intermittent and the mains were generally turned off at night and from Saturday night until Monday morning. So in 1846, despite some opposition, Sunderland Water Company was formed, adding South Shields to its operation eight years later.

Its first engineer was Thomas Hawksley, whose work became renowned throughout Victorian Britain. His work included designing the pumping station at Ryhope in 1869, now a scheduled monument, whose compound beam engines are maintained in working order by volunteers. It opens as a museum on bank holiday weekends and other special open days.

Hawksley's first waterworks was built on Humbledon Hill in 1846. Its distinctive pumping station has been converted into the region's first 'loft flats' as part of a 'brownfield' executive housing development of the type the council is encouraging on former industrial land.

A partnership involving the City Council, One NorthEast, English Heritage and the North East Civic Trust is leading a drive to promote other conservation-led regeneration of the old town, finding new uses for historic buildings and encouraging complementary new development. This builds on a longstanding policy in other areas where the preservation of grand Victorian terraces has been safeguarded by conservation regulations and where new uses have been found for old buildings. An outstanding example is Sunderland's first infirmary at the bottom of Chester Road, now part of the University of Sunderland, and more recently, the council has developed a managed office centre in the Edwardian River Wear Commissioners building in St Thomas Street.

Ryhope Waterworks and pumping station, now preserved as a museum, made an important contribution to health in the 19th century.

Opposite: St Thomas Street, the old River Wear Commissioners building, has been restored to its former grandeur.

RYHOPE WATERWORKS

chapter seven

Wearsiders at Play

These nylon swimming costumes were the height of fashion in the early 1950s.

BEACH TRIO

The "twin resorts" of Roker and Seaburn have been the playground of the people of Wearside for generations. Tastes in holidays may have become more sophisticated and exotic, but the first sign of summer still draws the crowds to the seafront.

So it's easy to forget that these "twins" have rather disparate ages. Roker developed first in the wake of the great transport revolution. Workers, enjoying their first taste of free time, travelled in from the pit villages and surrounding countryside on the new railways and Sunderland folk took one of the new trams from the town centre to the seaside in the latter half of the 19th century, but it wasn't until the 20th century that Sea Lane became the new resort of Seaburn further down the road.

Housing development was much slower than might have been expected, for the gentry preferred to build their grand houses in Ashbrooke rather than on the magnificent coastline over the river – for to reach it, they would have had to pass through the slums of Monkwearmouth.

However, some fine families did like it, including Cooper Abbs, solicitor to Sir Hedworth Williamson. The Abbs family lived at Rock Lodge, and the terrace of houses on the front at Roker and the Roker Hotel were commissioned by them in 1840. They were designed by John Dobson, the famous Newcastle architect.

The Roker Baths Hotel, as it was then known, flourished on the Victorian belief in the health-giving properties of sea water. Powerful pumping apparatus was introduced to pump sea water into the hotel to provide warm, cold, shower and vapour baths for the visitors. The cost varied between 6d (2½p) and 2s 6d (12½p) depending on the service and the time of day it was required. The hotel also provided sea bathing machines on the beach which cost 3d (1p) to hire and 6d if taken into the sea with a horse.

The first owner of the hotel was Edward Brown, who provided a horse and trap to convey visitors to and from the hotel via the country lane that connected the seafront via a country lane through Roker Farm, with the Brandling Junction Railway in Portobello Lane. (The last remains of the station, which served visitors travelling from Newcastle and the north, were removed in 1998.)

Access to the beach was assisted by the dumping of spoil from the building of the North Dock (whose engineer was Isambard Kingdom Brunel). The spoil created gentle slopes in place of the naturally steep limestone cliffs, then the pier and the lower promenade were built – though severe weather caused stoppages and the poverty-stricken workmen called a meeting in West Park to draw attention to their plight. But all the while, Seaburn remained undeveloped.

Cat and Dog steps at Roker taken in 1956.

Opposite: Edwardian and Victorian Wearsiders enjoyed the seaside
but kept covered up.

Postcards from the turn of the century demonstrate the popularity of Roker as a resort, but it's not until the 1920s that picture cards begin to show Seaburn. That stretch of coast wasn't part of Sunderland until Fulwell was taken over by the borough in 1928. In the next decade, promenades were constructed, the Seaburn Hotel (now redeveloped as the Swallow) and Seaburn Hall were built, along with a row of shops at Queen's Parade, and a home was found for the fairground.

The community spirit extended to the beach, with families, friends and neighbours meeting at their favourite spot. Entertainment included donkey rides along the beach and seaside shows by troupes like the Jumbles.

Religion played its part. Spotting the potential for conversion among the huge crowds, an annual Sands Mission began, with headquarters at St Andrew's. And Roker Sunshine Corner was popular, with its catchy signature tune: "Come and join us, come and join us, Roker Sunshine Corner is the place to be." There were other groups, too. A crowd of 500 gathered in May 1934, to watch Pastor Entwisle and his assistant, in black rubber vestments, carry out baptism by immersion.

Many people think the explosion of catering establishments along the seafront is an entirely new phenomenon. In fact it's a renewal of the former popularity of Roker and Seaburn as places to eat out.

Real Italian ice cream arrived at Seaburn in 1923 with Benedetto Notarianni who also had parlours in Silksworth Row and High Street West. Then there was Guidi's ("the Central Cafe of the Front"); Metcalfe's Ideal Cafe (which offered "tents, chairs and everything for the beach"); Atkinson's Seaburn Cafe ("luncheons, teas, suppers, party catering at moderate charges a speciality") and The North of England Cafe at Roker ("special accommodation for schools and choirs"). The history of Lockhart's cafe building, on the lower promenade at Roker, is a microcosm of changing tastes in entertainment. It was later the Beach Cafe, then several night clubs in succession and is now a pub.

Dreams of creating another Blackpool kept recurring in the 1950s and 1960s but Seaburn, with its boating pond, miniature railway, fairground and cafes on Queen's Parade, retained an almost Edwardian charm until the 1980s redevelopment incorporating a new hotel, sports centre and restaurant, amusement arcades and supermarket.

Now, sophisticated restaurants, year-round watersports like windsurfing and canoeing, a marina and new headquarters for Sunderland Yacht Club, offer pleasures undreamt of by Victorian day trippers. Today's swimmers, however, usually prefer the city's indoor leisure centres which house a full range of sports facilities.

Sailing, once a principal occupation of the menfolk of Sunderland, is now a popular hobby at Sunderland Marina.

Opposite: Excellent facilities such as the Marina and Yacht Club are attracting top televised sailing events to the City including the UK 18ft Skiff Grand Prix.

SUNDERLAND MARINA

Fears over the future of Sunderland's pubs in the 19th century seem to have been unfounded and some of the establishments in which the Victorians imbibed are among the most historic buildings in the city today, still popular despite wine bars, nightclubs – and even libraries.

For in 1855, when a committee was set up to discuss the "propriety" of starting a public library in Sunderland, the publicans were against it to a man – this new leisure activity, reading books free of charge, could affect takings.

A public meeting in the Athenaeum was described by a reporter as the rowdiest he had encountered, "with Councillor Sidgwick of the Londonderry acting as fugleman for the trade".

The Victorian notion, held by both temperance movement and licensed trade, was that if people read books they wouldn't drink. The library lobby won the day, but there is no evidence to suggest that people now making the 1,500,000 visits to Sunderland libraries each year are all teetotal. The pubs survived.

Song taverns and "harmonic rooms" attached to inns and licensed premises created a lively social scene in 18th and 19th century Sunderland. The drinking classes were well catered for – by 1821 there was a pub for every 80 in the population. Much business was conducted in the back rooms of taverns, as commercial premises were few and far between until the mid-century.

Low Street – the short street behind the fish quay, below High Street East – once had 41 pubs. For this was the principal thoroughfare for the river, and first port of call for sailors and keelmen coming ashore. On the separate wharfs, outside the shipyards, glassworks, roperies and so on, the workers had their own pubs. More elaborate "gin palaces" appeared, but the pubs were the centre of social life for many workers. And so it remained, though the First World War brought restricted hours.

It was in the 1960s that Sunderland developed an amazing nightlife again. Wearsiders born in wartime or in the post-war baby boom made up for the austerity of their early years by becoming sixties swingers. So did many of their parents, enjoying themselves into the early hours in nightclubs and two swish ballrooms.

Casinos helped subsidise the fees for top artists right through the week. The nightspots were glamorous and the workmen's clubs – some of them spanking new – smartened up to put up a spirited competition. By the time Roker Park played host to the 1966 World Cup Finals, Sunderland could boast six nightclubs with live acts.

The Beatles came twice, other stars included the Rolling Stones, Sandie Shaw, Bill Haley and the Comets, Jethro Tull, Pink Floyd, The Who and Fleetwood Mac. Discos have taken over now.

The Beatles are among the top-class artists who have appeared at Sunderland Empire Theatre.

Opposite: The Edwardian Londonderry is still a popular pub and replaced a Victorian inn of the same name.

THE BEATLES

Sunderland's Edwardian Empire Theatre is the main venue for live entertainment in the city today. It survived the advent of talking pictures, television and bingo and in its day has made more comebacks than the artists who have appeared on stage.

And what a galaxy of stars there have been – the Beatles, Marlene Dietrich, top national and international touring companies, opera and ballet (including Margot Fonteyn in Sleeping Beauty), and further back, Laurel and Hardy, W. C. Fields in a juggling act and homegrown Bob and Alf Pearson. The Empire closed briefly, but reopened under council ownership on Boxing Day, 1959, with a pantomime.

Designed as a great variety theatre by local architects the Milburn brothers, the Empire was opened in 1907 by Vesta Tilley, "the best-dressed young man in the theatre", who made her name with songs like 'Following in Father's Footsteps' and 'Piccadilly Johnny with a Little Glass Eye'.

Vesta Tilley was no stranger, for Sunderland had a fine set of theatres worthy of her presence. The first opened in Drury Lane and was known simply as "the Theatre" because it was the only one. But by the end of the 19th century, music halls had mushroomed throughout the town.

As each new hall opened, extravagant claims were made for it. When the Theatre Royal opened (with "a laughable extravaganza") in Bedford Street, in 1855, it was billed as "one of the most complete and magnificent temples of drama in the kingdom".

The People's Palace, which opened in 1891 with Marinelli, the human puzzle and reptile impersonator as top of the bill, assured patrons that there would be no entertainment of a vulgar character. It attracted top artists like Fred Karno's Mumming Birds, which gave Charlie Chaplin his big break. The proprietor of the Wear Music Hall – "the largest and most magnificent in Europe" according to an 1876 programme – was Stuart Henry Bell who valued himself highly as a scenic artist. He specialised in shows with a distinctive local flavour like Demon Spottee, the Cauld Lad and the Good Fairy of the Velvet Beds.

Churches and temperance organisations offered rival entertainment in a bid to keep their flock sober, but the pull of music hall was strong. Fierce competition kept prices down. Entrance in the early days was in "wet money", a refreshment check being given at the door to be exchanged for beer inside. When the "lion comique" roared out that "a merry quip and a cheerful shout are worth more than doctors round about", the audience was ready to believe him. And if any act failed to live up to the extraordinary claim made for it on the billboards, there was the added entertainment of hissing, booing and hurling missiles.

The magnificent interior of Sunderland's Edwardian Empire Theatre,
the main venue for live entertainment in the city.

INSIDE THE EMPIRE THEATRE

Supporting Sunderland AFC has been more a passion than a pastime for generations of Wearsiders, not something to be kept only for matchdays, but an abiding interest for everyday study and discussion. The 'Roker Roar' was a legend throughout the land, and now the club has transferred from the much-loved Roker Park to its top-class Stadium of Light, the volume of the roar seems to have reached new heights, rising across the river to reach shoppers in High Street whenever a goal is scored.

There have been plenty of spectacular goals and victories in the Premiership. Yet Sunderland supporters remain loyal and vociferous even in defeat and disappointment, of which there was more than a fair share in what became known as the "yo-yo" years following the club's first ever relegation in 1958. The high point came with the FA Cup victory in 1973, the all-time low in 1987 with a season in the Third Division. Fortunes fluctuated, loyalty never wavered. The day The Lads lost to Charlton in the 1998 play-off final for a Premiership place will be written on supporters' hearts for ever yet they choked back their disappointment to salute some of the most exciting football ever seen at Wembley.

Sunderland won six Championships before the Second World War and relished the proud record to be the only club never outside the top flight until that black day in 1958 when The Lads were relegated.

The club was founded in 1879, was elected to the Football League (founded in 1888) in 1890 and was dubbed "The Team Of All The Talents" by the League founder William McGregor. The team won the League Championship three times in four seasons between 1892 and 1895 and reached the FA Cup semi-final three times in the same period.

The team played at a number of different grounds before the opening of Roker Park on September 10, 1898. A pair of steamboats paraded up the river and a procession headed by a pipe band from the town to the ground preceded the grand opening by the Marquess of Londonderry.

In a team full of greats, top scorer Johnnie Campbell stood out. Since then, even when victory eluded them, Sunderland attracted some of the great players of all-time: Charlie Buchan in the 1920s; Raich Carter, after whom a new leisure centre has been named at Hendon; Bobby Gurney, Johnnie Mapson and Patsy Gallacher in the 1930s, when the elusive FA Cup was added in 1937 to League Championships; and after the war, in the high-spending Bank of England Club, Trevor Ford, Billy Elliott and Len Shackleton. Goalkeeper Jimmy Montgomery (Monty the Cat) was the hero of 1973. Now Kevin Phillips, Niall Quinn and manager Peter Reid will surely become legends in their turn.

One of the great moments of Sunderland AFC was winning the 1937 FA Cup, held aloft here by Raich Carter.

Opposite: Young supporters celebrate outside the gates of the Stadium of Light.

1937 CUP FINAL

chapter eight

A Century in Sunderland

The popular hot potato man was a familiar figure in Bedford Street for many years.

POTATO JOE

The 20th century opened with Sunderland confident of its position in the world. The Victorian merchants and industrialists who had made their fortunes in the industrial revolution of the 19th century, had created a gracious town centre.

In 1900, it was a shopper's paradise, and even boasted the largest department store outside London, Calvert's, in High Street. By then, following the building of the railway bridge and the Central Railway Station in Union Street in 1879, Fawcett Street was confirmed as the commercial heart. Grand residences had been converted to shops and offices, and purpose-built premises constructed in varied architectural styles, whose detail can still be seen in upper storeys above modern frontages. Most flamboyant of these is the Elephant Tea House, designed by Frank Caws in Hindu-Gothic style, and now housing a bank. Fawcett Street still has several classical bank buildings, but other landmarks like the Queen's Hotel which sent porters to meet every train, and the grand Town Hall, opened in 1890, have now gone.

One of the first great events of the century was the electrification of the tramways, newly taken over by the Corporation. The first electric tram left the Town Hall in August 1900 and the network spread quickly to both suburbs of grand houses for the gentry and new working class districts of distinctive single-storey terraced cottages. The first council houses were built in the overcrowded East End in 1903, but shortage of land there hampered the council's aim to clear the worst of the 19th century slums.

Another great event was the granting of the Freedom of Sunderland to Wearsiders returning from the Boer War. They included Captain Ernest Vaux, of the local brewery, who named an ale after the Maxim gun.

The early years were of continued boom, and Sunderland was secure in its claim to be the greatest shipbuilding town in the world. But by 1906 there was slump, bringing misery to workers laid off not only by the shipyards, but also by the vast array of other industries dependent on shipbuilding. Fortunes continued to fluctuate until the First World War, which saw the yards working at full stretch, building 300 vessels, mostly merchant ships.

Several emergency hospitals were set up in large houses, and a 600-bed hospital, forerunner of today's Royal Hospital, opened in Chester Road in 1917. The losses were grievous. The Wearsiders who volunteered for service formed one major brigade, one battalion and units of other regiments. Of the 1,000 Sunderland men who joined the 20th Battalion, Durham Light Infantry, more than 700 were killed or wounded. Those who survived were promised a "land fit for heroes to live in".

The first electric tram ready to leave the Town Hall in Sunderland in 1900.

FIRST ELECTRIC TRAM

Wearsiders turned out in their thousands to celebrate the end of "the war to end all wars". Of all the entertainments laid on in Sunderland for the peace celebrations on July 19, 1919, the greatest was the procession which wound its way round the town. Local bands augmented the pomp and ceremony of regimental bands with fife and drum, detachments of ex-servicemen were punctuated with floats representing historical characters.

People turned out on every street to celebrate the peace they thought would last forever. Hopes of prosperity were short-lived. World depression brought poverty and industrial unrest to Wearside in the inter-war years. Soup kitchens opened in the poorest areas and there were collections to buy boots for barefoot children. Some Wearsiders took advantage of assisted passages and sailed off to start a new life in Australia and Canada.

Those who stayed faced continuing unemployment. Only 17 ships were launched in 1923, the lowest tonnage output since the depression of the 1870s. By 1926, only eight of the 14 shipyards were still open. Attempts to cut wages, beginning with the coal industry, brought the General Strike. This collapsed on May 12, after nine days. The miners, with their slogan "Not A Penny Off The Pay, Not A Minute On The Day", held out until the end of the year.

Public projects, like the building of the new Wearmouth Bridge on the site of the old, in 1929, provided intermittent work. The building of Corporation Quay in 1934 also cleared some of the worst slums. But there was growing bitterness at the means test, the stringent investigation into a family's circumstances to determine whether unemployment benefit should be paid, and also at the labour camps to which local men were sent for hard physical toil. Sunderland had a large branch of the National Unemployed Workers' Movement. The Jarrow Crusade is the most famous, but there were many other marches and protest rallies.

Wearside, with its high unemployment and grinding poverty, was regarded as a key battleground by British Fascists in the 1930s, but they reckoned without the strong, decent working class culture of the area. Mosley's Blackshirts were greeted with derision, an extra-large bodyguard was nicknamed King Kong and on one occasion the crowd besieged the Blackshirts in the railway station.

As ever, Wearsiders enjoyed themselves despite their poverty. There were bands in the parks, illuminations on the seafront and every area had its own cinema and dance-hall. Any excuse was good enough for a celebration – and 1937 was a great year. Sunderland won the League and the FA Cup and there was also the Coronation to celebrate.

Local children celebrate the Coronation of King George VI and Queen Elizabeth in 1937, dirty faces and raggy ganseys notwithstanding.

Opposite: Bands in the parks remain popular to this day.

1937 CORONATION

Wearside's unemployment problems were cured overnight by the outbreak of war with Germany. People worked flat out in the mines, shipyards, engineworks, roperies, and all the riverside industries and went home to wartime duties as ARP wardens and Home Guards. Old men worked on well beyond retirement age. Women coped with the food and clothes rationing as well as with war work. Many joined the Services, others left home to work in the Land Army or in munitions factories, but thousands of others took on hard, physical work in shipyards and heavy industry locally.

Schools stayed closed well into the autumn of 1939 and evacuation began. Within a month, 8,000 children and 2,000 adults left Sunderland, followed by 1,761 the following year. Most were away briefly, but some were never to return. The heartache of parting turned to heartbreak for some parents – nine local children were among 77 evacuees who perished when the Canada-bound liner, City of Benares, was torpedoed.

By land, sea and air, Wearsiders played their full part in the fight against Fascism, but this was a war when the civilian at home was also in the front line. Sunderland was a key industrial target for the Luftwaffe. The longest air raid alert – from 11.30pm to 5am – was on April 15, 1941. This was the night – less than a week after Binns store had burnt down – that the Victoria Hall and the Winter Gardens were hit. There were other terrible nights, the worst perhaps being on May 24, 1943, when 83 people were killed, 3,500 left homeless, a further 10,000 houses damaged, gas, water and sewerage services and every type of building hit – schools, churches, shops, warehouses and factories. In the course of the war, 34,500 homes were damaged with 1,267 casualties and almost 300 people killed. There were many acts of individual courage and heroism, and hours of digging through the rubble in the hope of finding victims alive.

People played hard, too. Sunderland's 17 cinemas opened on Sundays and ran continuous performances from early afternoon every day, there were twice-nightly performances at the Empire, and dancing in Black's New Rink and Wetherells, and countless local institutes and church halls. The council ran extensive Holidays at Home programmes in the summer.

Throughout the war there were fund-raising events like Spitfire Week, but no effort was more steady than that of the families who formed a support group for the 600 men of Sunderland's own 125 Anti-Tank regiment, captured by the Japanese in February, 1941. With the remains of their funds, they held a dance for the survivors in the Rink ballroom in January 1946, the last of the end-of-war celebrations which had begun with VE night dancing in Mowbray Park.

During the Second World War, women were called to work in the shipyards and heavy industries of Sunderland.

Opposite: Another little boy leaves home in the wartime evacuation.

The war had been won, but austerity was still the order of everyday life in the early post-war years. The full employment of wartime continued, but so did the scarcity of goods and rationing was still in operation. In the summer of 1946, even the beer began to dry up.

A top priority for the council was to push ahead with its postponed housing programme and the clearance of slum property in multiple occupation. In 20 years, the provision of another 20,000 council homes was to transform Sunderland. By the 1950s, prosperity became visible – in the clothes Wearsiders began to wear, in the well-filled shops, and most of all in the new housing estates. In the 1960s, the town's skyline gained some high-rise flats, but it was not until the end of the decade that Sunderland acquired its two crowning pieces of sixties architecture – the £4million octagonal Civic Centre, replacing the Town Hall which was demolished to great dismay, and, on the bomb site in the town centre, the new shopping precinct, forerunner of The Bridges.

The pedestrian precinct brought another westward drift to shopping, but Liverpool House still survived near the old commercial heart in the East End. Other fine department stores like Kennedy's and Blackett's with their bills sent up to the cashier in suction tubes, as in the old Co-op in Green Street, flourished among smaller shops. The two giants, however, were undoubtedly Joplings and Binns, both of which provided the town with purpose-built department stores in the 1950s. Joplings also provided the town with its first escalator.

Traffic patterns were changing, too. Sunderland lost two of its best-loved forms of transport, in the trams and the ferry which crossed from Monkwearmouth to Bodlewell Lane in the East End. The ferry got an emotional send-off with its last passengers singing Auld Lang Syne as they crossed the river. New bus routes circled housing estates, linking them to the town centre, and more Wearsiders had their own cars. Congested roads were becoming a problem.

Wearside was still dependent on mining and other traditional heavy industry. In the 1950s, a quarter of men over 15 worked in shipyards and related industry, and 18,000 Wearsiders worked in pits. New trading estates with bright new factories opened up, but many of the new jobs were for women, who were entering the workforce in increasing numbers. Changing working practices meant fewer men were needed in the yards, mines and docks, and coal shipments were dropping. Although there was not the mass unemployment of the 1930s, the jobless figures stayed well above the national average in the 1970s, worsening in the 1980s.

Traffic congestion became a problem in the post-war years as this picture of Fawcett Street in 1953 shows.

Opposite: Victorian lamp-posts outside the old Town Hall in the 1950s.

FAWCETT STREET

Sunderland had suffered many blows in its history, but the last 20 years of the 20th century put the city's resilience to the test as never before. Decline and job losses were followed by the demise of entire industries. The 1980s and 1990s saw the traditional industrial fabric of Sunderland torn apart. It would have been easy to see further decline and decay as inevitable; instead, the city demonstrated an ability to adapt to new markets and survive against the odds.

The one piece of really good news on the industrial front was the arrival of car giant Nissan, which chose Sunderland against bids from elsewhere in Britain and Europe. Its role in the 21st century city is dealt with in the next chapter.

Yet no-one should underestimate the sadness, particularly among those most closely involved, at the loss of industries which were once the pride of Wearside. Doxford's engine works, once an unassailable giant dominating the world market, went in 1984. Shipbuilding, which had survived for 650 years on the banks of the Wear, disappeared in 1988. Wearmouth Colliery, the last of all the coal mines on which so much prosperity had been built, was closed down in 1993.

The Pallion craneworks, latterly Grove and before that Coles and Steels, ceased production in 1998. Its rugged, dependable mobile cranes could be found performing demanding tasks in some of the most inhospitable terrain in the world. But as with so much else, world renown was not enough to save it.

Then, in the last year of the century, Vaux brewery closed, ending a tradition spanning 160 years. It struck at the very heart of the city, physically and emotionally. Many felt the brewery had been sacrificed on the altar of big business, its fate decided by people who knew nothing of Sunderland or of what Vaux meant to the city. The campaign to save Vaux, led by managing director Frank Nicholson, whose family had long played a prominent role in the life of Sunderland, won the support of both individual Wearsiders and big local organisations. But the brewery went and with it, the fine Percherons which pulled the drays, adding colour and tradition to the city streets.

Another blow at the heart of the city came when Binns, with its giant department stores facing one another across Fawcett Street, closed in 1993. Shop At Binns For Everything – that had been the legend on every Sunderland bus, and on every tram before that. Founded in Sunderland in 1811, the Binns empire had eventually stretched the length and breadth of the country.

Against so much loss, what could be done to bring jobs and pride back to the Wear? The answer lay in a change of direction to take us into the next Millennium.

Percheron horses pulling Vaux drays added colour to the streets of Sunderland for more than a century.

Opposite: Shipyard cranes once dominated the skyline.

VAUX DRAYS

chapter nine

A City for the 21st Century

These six local people were winners of a competition to become a face of Sunderland 2000. They were selected from a flood of entries to promote the warmth and friendliness of the City world-wide.

Left to right: Balinder Sangha, Jayne Stout, Edwin Mason, Judy Sunley, Michael Thurlbeck, Dominic McDonough.

FACES OF SUNDERLAND

The pace of change gathered momentum in the closing years of the 20th century so that Sunderland entered the new Millennium with a new image. The fight to save traditional industries had been long and hard, and it had been lost. All energy could then concentrate solely on attracting new jobs.

The success of Nissan – by the end of the century, the most productive car plant in Europe – attracted a host of component manufacturers. The scene was set for the city to become a major automotive centre, hosting a major international conference for the industry. Now, 12,000 people are employed in the automotive industry in Sunderland.

The demise of shipbuilding and mining brought new efforts to restore and improve the environment. Enterprise Zone status brought incentives like rates holidays and a streamlined planning process to bring new firms in. The City Council administered two areas close to the A19, at Castletown, where the Sunrise Enterprise Park was set up, and at Doxford Park, where Doxford International Business Park is now world-famous. Hylton Riverside and the former Southwick shipyard site was administered by the Tyne and Wear Development Corporation, which in its reign brought a new riverside environment attractive for housing, leisure and industry. It set up business parks on the sites of the former Hylton Colliery and Southwick shipyard, developed waterfront housing and landscaping and a marina.

Another organisation established to give advice and practical help to start-up firms and provide training opportunities for people of all ages is the Sunderland Training and Enterprise Council, based at the Sunderland Enterprise Park. A key achievement was the setting up of the Business and Innovation Centre.

The split-site City of Sunderland College also rose to the challenge presented by the restructuring of industry. Once a training ground in skills needed by heavy industry, the College restructured its courses to meet new needs.

Sunderland placed itself at the cutting edge of the telecommunications revolution. As home to the only UK teleport outside London with World Teleport status, the city now ranks among world leaders in the field, like New York and Tokyo. Sunderland is now also one of the fastest growing call centre locations in Britain, attracting big names like Barclaycall, One2One and London Electricity. Thousands of people are now employed in dealing with customer enquiries by telephone and computer.

All this has been achieved with the City Council working in partnership with various agencies, including the Northern Development Company, now superseded by One NorthEast. A determination to find replacement industries for those that had gone saved the city from certain decline.

Nissan at Sunderland – the most productive car plant in Europe.

Opposite: London Electricity's call centre at
Doxford International Business Park.

NISSAN

A new corridor of opportunity in which the port and riverside will again play a key role, this time in a cleaner, greener environment, will take the transformation of Sunderland another giant step further in the early years of the 21st century.

Exciting new schemes include a riverside park and possibly a festival hall to enhance the £200million redevelopment of the city centre. It builds on other examples of an imaginative approach to breathe new life into areas hard hit by changes in traditional industries. People in Washington, for example, are benefiting from the new learning and leisure facilities at the new Millennium Centre, the first of its kind to open in the UK, and in Houghton a major programme of redevelopment is transforming the town centre, with work on the conservation areas winning three top design awards.

The new ARC of Opportunity programme is the latest major strategic initiative designed to help attract millions of pounds of business investment and create thousands of new jobs. The ARC (Area Regeneration Compact) turns the tragedy of closure of old industrial sites into new opportunities for investment.

Covering an area from the A19 in the west to the coast and including areas such as Pennywell and Hendon, the high profile programme will help focus Government attention on Sunderland. The initiative took its first step forward with a Government cash grant of £10.4million for Ford and Pallion. Major brownfield redevelopment opportunities include the port and railway sidings, sites that were once home to Grove and Vaux, Hendon Industrial Park and the possible expansion of Pennywell Industrial Estate.

The largest redevelopment opportunity is on the site of the port. Covering 270 acres, it is the second largest municipal port in the country. One NorthEast has funded a marketing and technical study to establish market demand for a redeveloped port, and investment proposals have been submitted.

The former Grove site is a prominent riverside location covering 100 acres and eventually will be adjacent to the Metro extension. On the other side of the river, Stadium Park covers an area of 50 acres, including the Stadium of Light and next to it, a nine-acre site being marketed with a wide brief including commercial, leisure and football-related development.

The 15-acre Vaux site stands right at the commercial and physical heart of the city and its future could have a major influence on the nature of development in the north west of the city centre. It is adjacent to the council-owned Galley's Gill area earmarked as a festival park with a hall and, with its low gradient riverside access, possibly another marina to cater for the growing demand in water sports.

This aerial view shows part of the ARC of opportunity along the riverside – the Area Regeneration Compact, a new initiative forged by the City Council in partnership with the Government, One NorthEast and key local agencies, will lead revitalisation of a 1,700 hectare area.

Opposite: The restoration of Church Street is part of the City Council's five-year programme of improvements to Houghton Town Centre. The project was funded by the Government's Single Regeneration Budget and the European Regional Development Fund.

VIEW FROM THE AIR

Past, present and futuristic new buildings all come together to provide stunning visual impact and variety at the heart of Sunderland city centre as it undergoes a major transformation. Victorian street furniture and cobbles enhance some of the older streets in the central conservation area, while elsewhere new buildings on clean minimalist lines demonstrate the best of modern architecture and design. Gone is the traffic congestion, noise and pollution of the past, as the city centre has been gradually pedestrianised, with only buses and hackney carriages using the main central streets. Pavements have been widened and new floral features added to increase the pleasure of simply strolling through.

Sunderland's new Park Lane Transport Interchange is already creating a positive first impression for people arriving in the city. Now one of the UK's busiest stations, with 15,500 buses running through each week, it has been designed to bring together buses, coaches and, by the end of 2001, the Metro under one canopy. The Metro will run every ten minutes and the Northern Spirit Newcastle and Middlesbrough express train service every 30 minutes.

Shopping is a major leisure activity for families today, and the aim of new developments has been to make sure that Sunderland can compete with the facilities of neighbouring rivals for variety and quality of goods. The shopping areas have been split into zones, each with its own identity with new names and themes and additional attractions like street entertainment.

One of the major success stories of the late century was the revamping of The Bridges shopping centre, attracting 350,000 visitors a week. Now the new extension doubles its size to 47,844 square metres with developments to the west of Crowtree Road fully integrated in the expanded centre. In keeping with development around it, the Crowtree Leisure Centre has undergone a £1million facelift with improvements including a ground level entrance, new reception area and new sauna suite.

A new multi-storey car park, with 740 spaces and attractive external brickwork, was the first structure under way and is designed to link directly to the centre. Debenhams is the largest of the new shops opening up. Three storeys high and built to a light, airy design, the store will bring its own fashion brands and exclusive designs. Other major retailers will include a range of outlets from fashion and accessories to sports gear.

Further plans including multi-screen cinema development are in the pipeline. The aim is to secure a safe, vibrant city centre catering for all tastes and age groups, with street trading, activities and entertainment day and night.

The new transport interchange at Park Lane provides a positive first impression to people arriving in the city.

Opposite: Debenhams – one of the biggest stores in the expanded shopping centre.

TRANSPORT INTERCHANGE

Nowhere will Wearside's heritage be more inextricably bound up with 21st century ideas and development than in Mowbray Gardens, which will be the jewel in the crown of Sunderland city centre for many years to come. Mowbray Gardens is the new umbrella name for Sunderland Museum and Art Gallery, the new Winter Gardens and Mowbray Park, although each retains its own name and identity in the new multi-million pound scheme, supported by the National Heritage Lottery Fund, to create a haven of culture and horticulture at the heart of the city.

The phased opening, starting in spring 2000, will gradually reveal the different facets of the scheme. The park is being restored to its Victorian glory and will include a rose arbour, fountains and other water features in the lake. The North Terrace has been redesigned to allow for its new role for evening use and entertainment – but the much-loved lions and balustrade will be back, cleaned and restored. In keeping with the policy of providing public art throughout the city, there will be a number of new art features in the park.

The Winter Gardens will take the shape of a glass rotunda and the exotic plants within will be able to be enjoyed from various viewing points, including a high level walkway inside. Palm trees will create an exotic canopy at the top of the dome, smaller trees and herbaceous plants will provide a shrub layer and then there will be a beautiful ground-covering display below. The planting scheme has been designed to provide year-round interest.

The Winter Gardens will be linked directly with the Museum which will have a Museum Street running through to a new glass level entrance from Burdon Road. Comfortable new facilities for visitors include a brasserie.

While the popular ship-building and coal galleries will remain, there will be many new galleries bringing Sunderland's rich heritage to life in exciting new ways. One of the most spectacular new items will be a large model of St Peter's monastery, which will form part of a new archaeology gallery with hands-on displays. In the new geology gallery, visitors will meet some of Sunderland's earliest inhabitants, including the world-famous Hetton Gliding Reptile.

The history of the city during the 20th century will be told through the eyes of ordinary people. Age-old textile craft skills like quilting, mat-making and gansey knitting will be on show. And the new Time Machine will include the first Nissan Bluebird built in the city as well as old favourites like Wallace the Lion, who will be joined by Wallace Junior and an automated Wallace who will roar when the clock strikes.

Model of the glass rotunda of the Winter Gardens.

Opposite: The new entrance to the Museum complements the old Museum's architecture.

WINTER GARDENS

Sunderland had long had the characteristics of an ancient city, with its proud place in the history of civilisation dating back to Anglo-Saxon times. But it was perhaps auspicious after all that it was not until 1992 that we were finally granted city status, for by then we were set fair to become a forward-looking city for the 21st century.

Colin Sinclair, the city's chief executive, who has overseen a dramatic transformation since his arrival in 1993, points out that the heavy industry which dominated the scene from the industrial revolution to the latter years of the 20th century, was in fact a relatively short period in the city's long history.

He believes that with the reclamation of old industrial land, and the restructuring of the economy with new hi-tech jobs based around business parks, the city is poised for a new post-industrial phase. He aims to ensure that the people of Sunderland have a key role in forging the future, as new systems of local government are put in place to engage communities more directly in plans to shape their destiny.

New investment and jobs will boost Sunderland's profile nationally and internationally, and increasingly, a new industry – tourism – will play an important role in the economy. Already the city is being marketed for city breaks and major events, such as Sunderland International Airshow which attracts one million visitors each year.

Looked at through the eyes of a tour brochure, the attractions are superb. The new waterfront, with the new university campus, top new restaurants such as Brasserie 21 and excellent new leisure facilities, reflects the changes in Wearsiders' lifestyles. Facilities include the Sunderland marina and yacht club, which attract high-profile national sailing events and put the city on the map as a first-class sailing venue.

The Stadium of Light towering above the banks of the Wear, regularly attracts capacity crowds and thousands of visitors from all over the UK and abroad. The National Glass Centre, offering a unique blend of industry and art, is becoming a focus for glass and glassmaking in Britain.

New developments like the new Winter Gardens, will alter the way people see the city. Physical changes go hand-in-hand with the deliberate re-structuring of our economy and public works of art are built into every new regeneration project. The City's Northern Gallery for Contemporary Art, housed within the award-winning City Library and Arts Centre, is the biggest contemporary arts space between Leeds and Edinburgh.

All this will attract increasing numbers of tourists as well as investment and jobs. But above all, it will improve the quality of life of the people who live and work here and who have made the city what it is today.

When Bishopwearmouth Parish Church, dating from the 12th century, became a Minster in 1998 it was believed to be the first created since the English Reformation. The Bishop of Durham, the Rt Rev Michael Turnbull, said it was an affirmation of Sunderland's success as a city and a symbol of "sure and certain hope for the future".

Opposite: Red-and-white interior of the Stadium of Light. The design helps the roar of the crowd reverberate round the ground.

SUNDERLAND MINSTER

postscript

As the Venerable Bede played a crucial role in establishing the Christian calendar, by which time is now marked the world over, it is fitting that the site of his monastery, on the banks of the Wear, should have been chosen as the starting point of the torch which lit the way to the new Millennium – not only in Sunderland but in the entire country.

The Beacon Millennium Flame used by the Queen to light the national beacon on the Thames was first kindled at Christian celebrations before a crowd of 25,000 worshippers at the Stadium of Light in May 1999. Flames from it were used to light early celebrations both in Northern Ireland and mainland Britain, and on New Year's Eve, to fire beacons throughout the country.

The Millennium Flame itself was housed within a glass torch created by Roger Tye at Phoenix Hot Glass Studio in the National Glass Centre. It was on this riverside site that glassmaking was first introduced to Britain by the abbot Benedict Biscop when he founded his monastery at Wearmouth in the seventh century. The torch was taken into St Peter's Church and on December 29, 1999, it was carried out by the Mayor, Councillor Ross Wares, under the Anglo-Saxon arch through which Bede and Biscop and all the important figures in medieval Christendom walked to worship. From here the Mayor took it to London where he handed it over to Keith Hill MP, Minister of London. It was given a formal reception by the Coldstream Guards who kept it safe until it was time for the Queen to light the national beacon on the eve of the Millennium.

So in a very real sense, the significance of Bede, the man who gave us the Millennium, was acknowledged at the dawning of the new age. And although a spectacular display of fireworks lit up the night sky over Penshaw Monument to mark the striking of midnight and the start of the year 2000, it was on Bede's riverside that families gathered to celebrate earlier in the afternoon. Here, with age-old symbolism, twelve young people carrying huge paper lanterns with images reflecting the changing face of the city, welcomed the future.

This book began on the riverside site which was one of the greatest centres of learning in Europe in the seventh century – and it ends with an image of the same site on the eve of the year 2000. Against the backdrop of the illuminated Wearmouth Bridge, Wearsiders welcomed the new Millennium with a family celebration along the riverside.

Opposite: The Mayor of Sunderland, Cllr Ross Wares, presents the unique glass torch carrying the Beacon Millennium Flame, to the Minister of London, Keith Hill.

LIGHTING THE FUTURE

acknowledgements

This book is a joint publication by the City of Sunderland and the Sunderland Echo.

City of SUNDERLAND

Sunderland Echo

Thanks are due to the following for help, advice and material used in this book: Phil Hall, Geoff Milburn, Stuart Miller, Andrew Bewick, Rob Ford, Paul Larkin, Gilbert Johnston, Doreen Talbot, Maureen Thompson, Nadine Hudspeth, Julie Elliott, Neil Sinclair, Martin Routledge, staff at Sunderland Museum, Tyne and Wear Museums Service, Tyne and Wear Archives, Sunderland City Library.

Photographs and illustrations in this book come courtesy of individual photographers, including Albert Snell, winner of a City Council competition, whose photographs are featured on pages 39 and 69. Other images are from collections at Sunderland Museum, Tyne and Wear Museums Service, Tyne and Wear Archives, the Artists Agency, Sunderland City Library, City of Sunderland, and the Sunderland Echo.

Public artworks featured on pages 9, 42 and 43 in this book are by Chaz Brenchley, Karl Fisher, Craig Knowles and Colin Wilbourn.

sponsors

We would like to acknowledge and give special thanks to the following leading organisations within the City of Sunderland who generously supported the production of this book.

AKELER

berghaus

City of Sunderland College

leighton

LONDON ELECTRICITY

NISSAN

REG VARDY plc

TRW

University of Sunderland